Vision in Progress

Vision in Progress

FRAMING THE PORTRAIT OF INDIAN BAPTISTS IN SOUTH AFRICA

RODNEY RAGWAN

RESOURCE *Publications* • Eugene, Oregon

VISION IN PROGRESS
Framing the Portrait of Indian Baptists in South Africa

Copyright © 2011 Rodney Ragwan. All rights reserved. Except for brief quotations in critical publications or reviews, no part of this book may be reproduced in any manner without prior written permission from the publisher. Write: Permissions, Wipf and Stock Publishers, 199 W. 8th Ave., Suite 3, Eugene, OR 97401.

Resource Publications
An Imprint of Wipf and Stock Publishers
199 W. 8th Ave., Suite 3
Eugene, OR 97401

www.wipfandstock.com

ISBN 13: 978-1-60899-557-8

Manufactured in the U.S.A.

*To my brother and brother-in-laws who are in pastoral and
Christian ministry:
Derryll Ragwan, Jebez Ragwan, Stanley Naidoo, Kennedy
Govender, and Cedric John*

Contents

Foreword by Rev. Dr. J. Jayakiran Sebastian / ix
Preface / xiii
Acknowledgments / xv
Abbreviations / xvi
Introduction / xvii

1 "Shine on, Lone Star!" / 21
2 South Africa's First Indian-born Missionary / 25
3 John Rangiah's Theology and Model of Mission and Ministry / 36
4 Following in John Rangiah's Footsteps / 52
5 Schism in the Indian Baptist Church / 58
6 Women in Ministry within the BASA / 63
7 The BASA and Unity Talks / 71
8 The BASA and the South African Baptist Alliance / 101
9 Ministry Strategies of the Baptist Association of South Africa / 120

Bibliography / 151

Foreword

RODNEY RAGWAN'S WORK OFFERS us much to think about not only because of the way in which local history is rediscovered, valorized, and validated, and also in terms of bringing to light documents, people, incidents, issues and themes considered peripheral to the "grand narrative." While the broader depiction may be important, one should never forget the very many brush-strokes that go into the so-called "big" picture. At the same time, while there may be much to admire when one steps back and takes a wide-angle view of a so-called "finished" product, one ought never to trivialize the "small" details that have played a significant, but often underappreciated, role in contributing to the ongoing task of enhancing and enriching the body of knowledge.

The history of the church has been a process of tracing the movements of people, movements that resulted in the encounter between the gospel as embodied in the lives of people who themselves were the products of particular locations and geography, and the local situations and cultures where new ways of embodiment and interculturation took place. The late missiologist-historian, Ogbu Kalu, wrote: "Christianity is implicated in a major global trend and yet, in the long run, global processes are multi-directional cultural flows that bedevil easy analysis."[1]

It is to the credit of Ragwan that he has eschewed "easy analysis" of a complex moment in the history of the church in South Africa through this significant work which looks at how an expatriate community, which was part of a broad swathe of sometimes voluntary but often forced and involuntary movement of people across the colonized landscape of the

1. Kalu, ed., "Changing Tides," 23.

world, in this case people from India who carried with them their hyphenated religious heritage and their inter-religious spiritual imagination into an unfamiliar territory in Kwa Zulu Natal. There they struggled to establish themselves, faced questions regarding identity and hybridity, internecine conflicts from within, and challenges of relevance and faithfulness from without, and yet did not waver in their commitment to continue to bear witness to the central reality that gave them a sense of purpose and hope—ongoing faith in the promises of Christ as testified to in the scriptures.

Using the tools developed and articulated by postcolonial theory and practice, Ragwan asks vital questions and teases out unexpected answers with implications for historical research and missiological praxis. Given the reality that the Indian Baptist Church in South Africa emerged and grew under the emerging stranglehold of what would become full blown apartheid, the multifaceted positioning of the Indian community in South Africa vis-à-vis the black, white, and colored population is certainly instructive. Also, the story is not confined to the nineteenth and twentieth centuries, but an evocative analysis is also offered with regard to this church in the post-apartheid era and on into the twenty-first century and the world-wide ecumenical partnerships that the church has entered into.

"Blunt histories do not always meet with warm approval", writes the prominent historian Margaret MacMillan.[2] At the heart of this work lies a candid and frank appraisal of the work of Rev. John Rangiah, who moved from India to South Africa at the beginning of the twentieth century to work amongst those indentured laborers from India who arrived in South Africa as Telugu-speaking Baptists. The life and times of this fascinating personality make for compelling reading, not least the reconstruction of his contribution through pamphlets and memories among other source material, and with the researcher facing the reality of being denied the possibility of casting his scholar's net wider by certain vested interests, but being able to circumvent some of these imposed obstacles by other methods.

The work is framed by the social, political, and ecclesiological realities that directly and indirectly impacted the life of the small but thriving community under investigation. Often generic terms like "Baptist"

2. MacMillan, *Dangerous Games*, 41.

conceal the intricacies of what such terms evoke at various levels—local, national, and international. The writer has attempted to unpack the composite nature of this term and situate it in interplay between concept and context. Apart from all this the harsh realties of apartheid provoked a variety of responses to the deeper questions of human existence and human inequality. Although quite a lot of research has been done on the consequences of the Lutheran World Federation and the World Alliance of Reformed Churches declaring in the late 1970s and early 1980s that apartheid was a sin, the ground changes in various churches and church families in South Africa are only slowly being documented and analyzed. In this sense too, Ragwan's work offers us an indispensable view of the continuities, collaborations, changes, and challenges that this local Baptist community and what it developed into was confronted with, and how leaders like Rangiah, his descendants, and the communities of faith were impacted by, and in turn, impacted these realities.

Brian Stanley in his fine analysis of the World Mission Conference in Edinburgh held one hundred years ago in 1910 points out that "two intermingled voices" emerged from this conference. One was the voice of "boundless optimism and unsullied confidence in the ideological and financial power of western Christendom" and the other "more muted and discerning voice" was that which spoke of "crisis and opportunity, of challenge and competition, and occasionally even of threat and danger."[3] It is to Ragwan's credit that his nuanced and discerning voice has given rise to a fine work, something that will go a long way in attempting to restore balance to what has often been a one-sided and paternalistic style of missiological and ecclesiastical writing and analysis in this our interdependent world of ecumenical challenges and opportunities in a world where racism and colonial mentalities have not been obliterated, but lurk even amongst well-meaning and earnest researchers.

Rev. Dr. J. Jayakiran Sebastian
H. George Anderson Professor of Mission and Cultures
Director, Multicultural Mission Resource Center
The Lutheran Theological Seminary at Philadelphia

---

3. Stanley, *World Mission Conference*, 16.

Preface

THE UNBANNING OF THE liberation organizations, the release of Nelson Mandela, and the historic democratic elections in 1994 in South Africa ushered in a new dispensation for its citizens. Voices and stories that were once stifled and marginalized began finding their space in the public domain. At an International Missions Conference hosted by the Baptist Convention of South Africa in 1994 I was given the space to share-as well as to have people listen with interest and appreciation to-my history. For me this was very liberating. Such new found space and listening ears, as well as my own interest in my Christian heritage, motivated me to research more of my Baptist history.

My early understanding of the history of Indian Baptists and their arrival and mission in South Africa was largely informed by stories, sermons, brochures, and newsletters told and written mainly by my fellow South African Indian Baptists. These sources gave me a good foundation, but I felt I needed to uncover more. My inquiry led me to research sources in the USA and India. The sources in South Africa, USA, and India helped me to construct a missionary enterprise which spanned three continents: America, Asia and Africa.

The vision to send a missionary to India was birthed in the USA. When Indians experienced the Christian faith, they took it upon themselves to send their own missionary to South Africa to work among the indentured laborers in Kwa Zulu Natal (formerly known as Natal). In 1903 John Rangiah gave expression to that vision. A few other Indian-born missionaries followed the vision, and, I believe, went on to carve a place in the memory of South African Indian Baptists. However, the vision that was caught and developed by brown-skin Christians in the late nineteenth century is a rare read. Additionally, the birthing of that vision and telling of this story in South Africa was impeded by colonialism. The stories of people of color were not given the space in the history books. Additionally, during this period apartheid further marginalized such stories. It is time that these stories be told. In this book I tell of a vision that had its genesis in the USA, developed in India and was carried to and given expression in South Africa. I write how men and women believed that they could be not only a mission field but a mission force in world missions and who went ahead and did just that. Today, this vision is far from ideal. It is still being shaped; it is a vision in progress.

Acknowledgments

IN 1990, THE BRIGHT hope of a new tomorrow became a reality in South Africa. A new democratic country was born. During the dark and turbulent days of apartheid, I had friends who provided encouragement and inspiration. One such friend was Desmond Hoffmeister. Among other things, Desmond planted the seed in me to tell my faith story. I took him up on this. Later on, Jayakiram Sebastian, Samuel Chetti, and Daryl Balia tilled the soil and got me to pursue this project. Several family members and friends both in South Africa and in the USA assisted me with research, and encouraged me through this process: Noah Moses Israel, Derryll Ragwan, Richard Nathaniel, Brian Naidoo, T. Rhandram, N. Timothy, Cedric John, Kennedy Govender, Gail Randolph-Williams, Ruth McFarland, and Wallace Charles Smith. I am indebted to Randy Frame for assisting in editing the manuscript and improving the books readability. Special thanks to the staff at Wipf & Stock Publishers for their work. Thank you as well to Yeshodha Rajcoomar and Jenhell Caythen for being part of this experience. To my wife, Eva, and children, Renton, Edwin, and Renee go my heartfelt thanks and appreciation for their support and love. You played important roles in allowing the seed that was sowed years ago to bear fruit. Last but not least, I am thankful to God for strength, grace, and patience.

Abbreviations

ABC American Baptist Church
ABHMS American Baptist Home Missionary Society
BASA Baptist Association of South Africa
BCSA Baptist Convention of South Africa
BMSA Baptist Mission of South Africa
BUSA Baptist Union of South Africa
BRBM Bulwer Road Baptist Minutes
BWA Baptist World Alliance
BWAW Barkly West Awareness Workshop
CBM Colesberg Baptist Minutes
DEIC Dutch East India Company
KPC Kempton Park Consultation
HMS Home Mission Society
LAC Local Arrangements Committee
NIBA Natal Indian Baptist Association
SABMS South African Baptist Missionary Services
SBC Southern Baptist Convention
TBHMS Telugu Baptist Home Missionary Service
TRC Truth and Reconciliation Commission

Introduction

STORIES OF NON-WESTERN MISSIONS in the early nineteenth century were quite rare. Here is a story of how a brown skin Telegu Baptists from the subcontinent who was inspired by the vision of his fellow native Indian Baptist to go to South Africa to serve as a missionary. Almost 94 years later, this narrative was put into perspective missiologically and historically.

In the year 2000 I initiated a partnership between the American Baptist Churches, USA (ABC) and the Indian Baptist Church in South Africa. The following year I was invited by the ABC to attend an International Mission Conference in the state of Wisconsin. The conference focused on American Baptist missions around the world. It was here where I discovered that the ABC was in many ways responsible for the mission work in South Africa on which this book focuses.

This exemplifies how Baptist historians have not adequately documented South African Baptist Indian History. During my studies at a prominent Baptist institution in South Africa I discovered how little Indian Baptist history was addressed and reflected in the curriculum of a missions course. Furthermore the available mission history is, unfortunately, not fully and accurately represented in the historical records. What I learned in Wisconsin is just one of many examples of how the South African Indian Baptist history has been ignored.

The need to reclaim the history of Indian Baptist work in South Africa is due in large part to the multiple levels of colonization South Africa experienced and to three centuries of institutional racism there. At the heart of these two systems of oppression was the dehumanization of the peoples of Africa, Asia, and the Americas. This work is a historical narrative of the Baptist Association of South Africa (BASA), a predominantly ethnic organization in the province of Kwa Zulu Natal. It focuses on BASA's influence on the development of the Indian Baptist Church in South Africa. Again, the Indian Baptist narrative has not been given much attention by church historians. The available records appear in non-academic literature and are written mainly by laypersons with a few appearing in theses and dissertations.

As for the few academic writings that are in existence, they do not fully reflect the socio-political forces that influenced the marginalization of this narrative. My goal is to provide a post-colonial narrative of this history. In a world of post-colonial and post-modernist deconstruction of the meta-narrative, I propose a historical narrative of a particular people in a particular time.

Baptist mission in South Africa, as noted above, took place in the context of colonialism. Generally, in critiquing colonialism, scholars have almost always criticized the West. Sugirtharajah[4] contends that postcolonialism involves once-colonized "Others" insisting on taking their place as historical subjects. He further asserts that, unlike such "isms" as feminism and structuralism, postcolonial discourse is not about the West, but about the colonized "Other." The narrative of the Baptist Association of South Africa is that "Other." What sets my approach apart is its use of postcolonial hermeneutics to interpret the narrative.

This work focuses heavily on the work of John Rangiah, the founder of the Indian Baptist Church in South Africa. Rangiah was influenced by colonialism to some degree, especially with regard to his understanding of the Bible. However, when it came to mission, as will be seen, his was an indigenous approach. In addition, a critique of the colonial influence on Rangiah establishes that he was not exposed to the critical reflections on colonialism, either in his native India or in South Africa. By and large, the general membership of the current Baptist Association of South Africa has managed to insulate itself from the discourse generated by postcolonial critical theory.

This book includes an examination of Rangiah's understanding of the Bible and its themes, addressing questions surrounding the hermeneutical principles that guided his understanding and interpretation of the Bible. Interpreters have often relied on critical and literary theories as well as literary theories to interpret Scripture. Sugirtharajah[5] contends

---

4. Sugirtharajah, *Hermeneutics and Post-colonialism*, 16.
5. Ibid., ix.

that even social science methods have been applied to Biblical studies, but he points to a relative neglect of one of the most challenging, critical and controversial theoretical categories of this time, namely post-colonialism. I will examine the extent to which Rangiah and the Baptist Association of South Africa neglected such a critical category.

In Rangiah's defense, theology, according to M. Steele Ireland,[6] is a relatively new dialogue partner with post-colonial theory, though Ireland adds that the conversation is quickly developing. Rangiah, who was reared in one colonial context and came to another, did not have the opportunity to fully engage this postcolonial theory.

Rangiah represented a people who in India were influenced and divided by the caste system. I will critically examine claims that this phenomenon influenced Rangiah's ministry in South Africa.

Finally, this work will include an evaluative element, specifically a countering of the dominant Baptist history. I will describe and evaluate the sequence of events associated with the Baptist Association of South Africa in light of the transformation that is taking place in that country. Each of South Africa's four main population groups—Blacks, Whites, Coloreds and Indians—has a unique history.

Unfortunately, the histories of these people of color have been at least marginalized if not completely ignored. The colonial apartheid missiological paradigm made people of color believe that their "stories" were not important. Historians representing the dominant Baptist organization did not adequately include the contributions of Black, Colored and Indian Baptists. The history of South African Indian Baptists is submerged in that of white Baptists and is written from a colonial and paternalistic perspective. Thus, the impact and importance of that history has been skewed or minimized. And very little of it appears in the curricula of South African theological institutions.

Mark Taylor,[7] in his book *Altarity*, writes about the suppression of minority voices by the dominant forces. He suggests that the systematic exclusion of what he calls the "Other" will undoubtedly result in the politics of appropriation and domination. Indeed the BASA, a minority Baptist organization, suffered such a fate. Taylor[8] further contends that the written history of nineteenth century colonial mission has been

---

6. Dyrness and Kärkkäinen, ed., *Dictionary*, 683.
7. Taylor, *Altarity*, xxi.
8. Ibid.

predicated on various themes of subordination of ancient culture and socio-religious conversion of the colonized people. Additionally he states that subordination provided control over the silenced subjects.

The vast majority of the South African Indian population depended on the oral transmission of its history. This was done through storytelling and sermons. It is a history that has by and large been lost. Within the Indian Baptist church itself, not many took the initiative to document the contributions of Indians to the development of the Christian faith in South Africa. As suggested above, the few academics who did so have limitations, among which is the omission in their writings of the role of women. Consequently, the important role of women has not been fully recognized by the Indian Baptist Church in South Africa.

This book will include the contributions of American Baptists, the Southern Baptist Convention, and the Telugu Home Missionary Society in India. Rangiah's relationship with the ABC dates to their founding of a Baptist Church in India among the Telugu-speaking people. Some of his correspondence with this church is available in the ABC archives at Valley Forge, Pennsylvania, USA. The records of the Southern Baptist Convention's missionary work in South Africa among the Indians may also be accessed in Nashville, Tennessee.

The period covered in this book goes from the late 1800s to 2006. This book does not examine the narrative of the Baptist Mission of South Africa, another Indian Baptist organization with John Rangiah as the founder, although the history of the Baptist Mission of South Africa is part of the Indian Baptist history and shares a cultural and ethnic heritage similar to the BASA. Nor am I able to include the contributions of every leader of the Baptist Association of South Africa since its inception in 1903.

Since this narrative is written from church historical and missiological perspectives, it will take into consideration the effects of societal influences on the South African Baptist population, but will include historical analysis as well as a missiological and theological examination of the mission of South African Indian Baptists.

In sum, as a native of South Africa of Indian descent, I believe in the scholarly necessity of what Michel Foucault[9] refers to as "the insurrection of subjugated knowledge." I hope that this study will contribute to a better understanding of the theological, social, and cultural development the Baptist Association of South Africa made in South Africa.

9. Foucault, *Power/Knowledge*, 80–81.

1

"Shine on, Lone Star!"

Baptists from India Arrive in South Africa

THE YEAR 1853 WITNESSED a turning point in the history of the mission work among the Telugu people in India. After seventeen years of American Baptist Churches ministry among the Telugus, the viability of this ministry came under review at a Missionary Union board meeting held in Albany, New York. Reports from missionaries in India were not positive. However, the Missionary Union learned that this mission field had significant potential, as the missionaries working there had acquired the language. Also, their witness had resulted in a few converts. But the progress was minor, leading some to advocate handing the work over to other mission agencies.[1]

A proposition was made that a letter be written to Dr. Jewett, the American Baptist missionary in India, requesting that he close the mission and relocate to another mission in Burma. The board secretary, however, was reluctant to write this letter, and eventually refused to do so. When the Telugu Mission was discussed by the board, one of the speakers, in the course of his address, turned to the mission map that hung on the wall. He pointed to Nellore, the location where the Telugu Mission was established. The speaker called it the "Lone Star," as this was just one lonely mission in India.

---

1. Downie, *Mill to Field*, 46.

The Rev. S. F. Smith, author of the *National Hymn,* was present at this meeting. Before going to bed that night he wrote, as recorded by David Downie,[2] the following lines:

THE LONE STAR

> Shine on, "Lone Star!" Thy radiance bright shall spread o'er all the eastern sky; more breaks apace from gloom and night; Shine on, and bless the pilgrim's eye. Shine on, "Lone Star!" I would not dim. The light that gleams with dubious ray; The lonely star of Bethlehem led on a bright and glorious day. Shine on, "Lone Star!" in grief and tears, and sad reverse oft baptized; Shine on amid thy sister spheres; Lone stars in heaven are not despised. Shine on, "Lone Star!" Who lifts his hands to dash to earth so bright a gem, A new "lost plead" from the band that sparkles in night's diadem? Shine on, "Lone Star!" The day draws near when none shall shine more fair than thou; Thou, born and nursed in doubt and fear wilt glitter on Immanuel's brow. Shine on, "Lone Star!" till earth redeemed, In dust shall bid its idols fall; And thousands, where thy radiance beamed shall "crown the Savior, Lord of all."

The following day this poem was read at the board meeting. Many wept and sobbed as it was read. Whatever doubts the board had about the viability of the Telugu mission in India vanished. The board unanimously voted to reinforce the mission. Little did the board realize that this mission among the Telugus would someday have global implications. In fact, the Baptist Association of South Africa churches in South Africa are indebted to Dr. S. F. Smith for his contribution to the history of the Telugu Mission in India. The poem cited above is an important part of the history of the Baptist Association of South Africa.[3]

Instead of being abandoned, the work among the Telugus by American Baptist missionaries grew. One of the most significant developments was the initiative of the Telugus to establish their own indigenous missionary organization, called the Telugu Home Missionary Society. This happened in 1897, forty-four years after the Telugu mission was almost closed by the American Mission Union.[4] The vision of the new

---

2. Ibid., 47.
3. Ibid.
4. Rangiah, *Telugu Mission,* 1.

organization included sending its own native missionary, John Rangiah, to another country.

Rangiah[5] described the economic status of these Telugu-speaking Christians as extremely poor. Though many of them earned only a few pence a day, they decided in faith to participate in a global mission enterprise by sending one of their own as a missionary to what was then called the Natal province. The NIBA News[6] reported, "The Lone Star Church at Nellore was the happiest of them all, it was sending one of its cherished sons as the first Indian Baptist Missionary to a distant field." Given the economic status of these indigenous Christians and the uncertainty of life in Africa at the time, the action of the Telugu people to commit themselves to world mission is to be commended.

The immediate mission in Natal, South Africa was to provide spiritual services to indentured Baptist laborers there. In 1900 hundreds of Indian indentured laborers came to South Africa. Among them were about 150 Baptist Christians from Madras, India. These laborers came in response to the British authorities in Natal for Indians from India to enter into contract to work in the sugar and tea estate industries. According to the *Natal Mercury*, dated November 22, 1860, among this group were mechanics, household servants, domestics, gardeners, and trades people. There were also bankers, carpenters, and accountants among them. Many of the laborers were dispatched to the tea estates of Kearsney on the North Coast of Natal. Kearsney would become a significant location where Telugus established themselves under the leadership of John Rangiah.

Rangiah, the founder of the Telugu Baptist Church in South Africa, was in correspondence with the American Baptist Churches Foreign Mission Society in India. He provided the Society with progress reports on the work in South Africa among the Telugus, sharing the needs of its ministry as well as expressing thanks for the prayer support given by the Society.

The owners of the tea estates, the Huletts, had previously sought the assistance of Wesleyan missionaries for meeting the spiritual needs of their indentured laborers, who spoke very little English. Soon, language and denominational problems emerged; the Telugus found it challenging to relate to these Wesleyan missionaries. Baptist Indians expressed the desire to have a Telugu Baptist minister. In 1903, Rev. John Rangiah and

5. Ibid.
6. Rangiah, *NIBA News*, 9.

his family accepted the invitation to go to South Africa to work among the Telugu Indians.[7]

---

7. Israel, *History*, 5.

2

South Africa's First Indian-born Missionary

John Rangiah

FINETTE JEWETT[1] WROTE ABOUT John Rangiah's father's eagerness to receive an education. John's father, T. Rangiah, would consistently arrive at the American Baptist School in Nellore requesting the opportunity to learn. The Lymans, who were American Baptist missionaries in India, granted this request, recognizing that T. Rangiah was a diligent student. Consequently he was employed as a student to tutor others at the school. During his association with the American Baptist missionaries in Nellore, T. Rangiah converted to Christianity and later became the pastor of the Madras Baptist Church. T. Rangiah had four sons, all of whom became ministers.

There are no records revealing who was responsible for John Rangiah's conversion. American Baptists were probably instrumental. However, Rangiah[2] states that in the then Madras Presidency the Christians owed their conversion to the work of the American and Canadian missions.

It seems that John spent much of his boyhood around American Baptist missionaries. As a young man he took an active part in Christian ministry. He served as a Sunday School teacher, Sunday School superintendent, lay preacher, evangelist, treasurer and deacon. Rangiah also served as headmaster of the Nellore Boys School from 1897 to 1900 and

---

1. Jewett, *Leaves*, 49.
2. Rangiah, *Reports*, 1.

of the Nellore Girls School from 1901 to 1903. On April 20, 1903, he was ordained as a minister of the Lone Star Baptist Church.[3]

Mrs. Lyman Jewett[4] wrote in a journal an article titled "John Rangiah, The First Telugu Foreign Missionary" in which she records the life of Rangiah while in India and his work in South Africa. She provides a background of Rangiah's parents and their conversion to Christianity. She describes Rangiah's commitment to the Christian faith and, more specifically, to his personal life. She wrote[5] about Rangiah's prayer request, which he shared at his ordination service. He requested that the audience pray that he would not be proud, as he was the first foreign missionary and so many kind words were spoken of him. Lyman further refers to the positive comments of two important leaders about Rangiah's work in South Africa: David Downie and Dr. McLaurin, a professor at the Ramapatam Seminary in India. Dr. McLaurin shared the good work of Rangiah's ministry in South Africa, stating that it "has given a mighty impetus to the revival spirit in the seminary at Ramapatnam, and we shall extend it, if possible, into every church."

Rangiah made his decision to accept the call only after much prayer. The NIBA News[6] describes Rangiah's vision that confirmed his call. On January 24, 1903, he had a vision where he saw two angels who comforted him with the words, "We have been praying to the Lord for the past few years . . . that He may send a Telugu preacher and today He has provided one for us." The angels then handed him Bibles. Rangiah described this experience as "glorious." The NIBA News[7] recorded his response as, "Praise be to the Lord." He felt encouraged and assured of the direction he needed to take with regard to his ministry.

ARRIVING IN SOUTH AFRICA

Rangiah, his wife, Kanakamma, and two children, Manoharam and Premaleelah, left India for South Africa in May of 1903. Rev. Rangiah described the journey by ship to South Africa as follows:

3. Rangiah, *NIBA News*, 10.
4. Jewett, *Rangiah*, 1–6.
5. Ibid., 4.
6. Rangiah, *NIBA News*, 9.
7. Ibid.

> I, with my wife and two children, left Nellore on the 9th May 1903, and on 11th took passage by the steamer 'Safari'. After just amonth, i.e. on the 11 of June, we arrived at Port Natal and found shelter at the mission house of the South African General Mission.[8]

Rangiah continued by describing one of his earliest experiences upon arriving in South Africa. He was asked to visit a prisoner at a prison in Durban where the prisoner was waiting to be hanged. Rangiah spent an entire month visiting the condemned man. He presented the Christian faith to him. He recorded that moments before his hanging the prisoner remarked: "I go to the refuge at the feet of the Savior, Jesus Christ."[9]

Rev. Tomlinson, a white minister of the South African General Mission (SAGM) took Rangiah to Phoenix, Durban; Duffs Road; and Verulam, where he ministered to Indians. The SAGM attempted to persuade Rangiah to work with this mission organization, but Rangiah felt that his obligation was to the Telugus from Kearsney. He discussed with Mr. Walton of the SAGM his decision to go to Kearsney as well as his vision to start the Telugu Baptist Mission. A short while later, Rangiah felt the need to go to the people of Kearsney, first because it was at their request that he was sent to South Africa, and second to advance his vision of the Telugu Baptist Mission.

The SAGM suggested to Rangiah that the Telugu Baptist Mission be brought under the control of the SAGM; the SAGM promised to supplement his salary. After prayerful consideration Rangiah informed the SAGM in writing that he could not join them. He cited two reasons. First, the Telugu Baptist Home Mission Society of India had sent him to Natal and had not given permission to join with the SAGM; neither was the Society interested in handing its work over to SAGM. Second, for the little extra financial assistance and other material benefits he would receive, Rangiah did not want to dampen the enthusiasm and interest so far shown by the Home Mission Society in the Natal work. Rangiah was committed to the Telugu work in Natal, and set out to Kearsney to begin his mission.

At Kearsney, the Huletts, owners of the Kearsney Tea Estate, received the Rangiahs warmly. Sir Liege Hulett was greatly touched by the humility of the Rangiahs and their devotion to God. He gave them a large

---

8. Rangiah, *Reports*, 1.
9. Ibid.

house on his property. The generosity of the Hulletts moved Rangiah, who expressed great thanks to God, saying, "He raiseth up the poor of the dust and lifteth the needy out of the dunghill."[10] Mr. D. Benjamin, a Telugu Christian leader, met the Rangiahs as they made their transition from Phoenix, an Indian township near Durban, to Kearsney on the Natal North Coast. Benjamin, too, extended hospitality to the Rangiahs and helped them acclimatize to the new and different conditions in Kearsney.

The first Indian Telugu Baptist Church was formed on December 27, 1903 at Kearsney. Rangiah wrote to the American Baptist Foreign Mission Society about this historical development: "December 27th was a memorable day in South Africa, for on that Sunday we formed the first Telugu Baptist Church in this land. Sixty-four Telugu Baptist Christians, including myself and my wife, formed the church."[11]

Rangiah submitted annual reports of his work among the Telugus in South Africa to the American Baptist Foreign Missionary Society (ABFMS). He wrote about the approach he employed in his work among the Telugus. He also wrote about the missionary tours he undertook as he set about his mission work. These tours were typical of those made by the American Baptist Foreign Mission Society. Rev. Samuel Day, as well as Rev. Jewett,

American Baptist Missionaries in India, made similar tours of the villages where they accessed the needs and opportunities for evangelism.

In addition to the formal reports, Rangiah's communication with an American missionary and a letter to an internal mission magazine provide insight into his work and understanding of mission.

Rangiah, in his first and second annual reports on the Telugu Baptist Mission in Natal, described his visits to Phoenix.[12] He had gone there in search of Baptist Christians. He further reported on his visits to areas like Stanger on the Natal North Coast and then to Kearsney.

Kearsney became the headquarters of the Indian Telugu work in South Africa. According to Rangiah, he settled in Kearsney on October 9, 1903. Rangiah praised the landlords, Sir and Lady Liege Hulett, for their hospitality in providing them with a large house. He reported: "This liberal minded and benevolent gentleman takes a genuine and enthusias-

---

10. Ps 113:7.
11. Rangiah, *Reports*, 1–3.
12. Ibid., 4.

tic interest in enterprises pertaining to the Kingdom of Christ." Rangiah received rations as well as medicine for himself and his family.

The highlight of his reporting was the previously mentioned establishment of the first Telugu Baptist Church in South Africa. According to Rangiah, 64 members were part of this church that was established in Kearsney. The first harvest reaped was six new believers, who were baptized in the Umvoti River on February 14, 1904. A new name was given to this river by Rangiah. It was referred to as the Gundlacumma of Natal, with earnest hopes and prayers for the further progress of the Kingdom.[13]

Rangiah, a fellow Telugu who was familiar with the culture of the indentured laborers, began an Indian church with Indian leadership. He had a choice between two main Protestant strategies for the creation of indigenous churches, understood as churches suited to local culture and led by local Christians. The first is indigenization wherein foreign missionaries create well-organized churches and then hand them over to local converts. With this approach, the foreign mission is generally seen as a scaffolding that must be removed once the fellowship of believers is functioning properly. Missionaries provide teaching, pastoral care, sacraments, buildings, finance and authority, and then train local converts to take over these responsibilities. Thus the church becomes self-supporting, self-propagating, and self-governing.

The second strategy, indigeneity, is where foreign missionaries do not create churches, but simply help local converts develop their own spiritual gifts and leadership abilities and gradually develop their own churches. Missionaries provide teaching and pastoral care alone. The church is thus indigenous from the start.

Rangiah's approach was based on the indigenization strategy, thus he set out to use local leadership for the churches he started, enabling them to become self-supporting, self-propagating, and, to a certain extent, self-governing.

GROWTH AND EXPANSION

In reporting to the Foreign Missionary Society, began by revealing that the year under review, 1906, was successful but not without troubles, struggles, and hardships, both within and outside of the church. These challenges in-

---

13. The Gundlacumma is a river in South India, where 2,222 people, mainly Telugus, were baptized in one day.

cluded travelling to the various areas by horseback and raising funds for the support of Christian leaders. However, due to his strong faith in God and a resolute spirit, he remarked that the gracious spirit of the Lord followed him closely and that he was able to overcome every challenge.

Rangiah[14] wrote about his deep longing for revival among the Telugus. He recognized the obstacles to this revival and confronted them through the preaching of the Bible. He reported[15] that inside the church there were "secret sins being fondled." According to him, the leading members of the church were involved in sinful activities. There was also the issue of self-support for the other Christian workers. This impeded the spread of the gospel, wrote Rangiah, as members were being disillusioned. To add to these challenges, there were Zulu uprisings, which caused alarm and slowed their movements for months. In view of all that was happening with the work among the Telugus, Rangiah was convinced that what was required of them was a full surrender to the Lord and His will.

As a result of their strong emphasis on prayer, revival broke out. Rangiah reported that August 12, 1906 was a day of inexpressible blessing. A sermon was preached from Galatians 6:6–8. Prayer meetings followed at the home of one of the members, where people began weeping. Many cried aloud, and confessions of sins followed. According to Rangiah these prayer meetings carried on for more than four months. The churches established by Rangiah all began to experience similar revivals. A hill in Kearsney, the headquarters of the Telugu Baptist Mission, became a place of prayer as well. Many wanted to identify with Jesus when he went away from the crowd to be alone in prayer.

Rangiah reported on the five churches he established in Natal, South Africa. They were Kearsney, Verulam, Darnall, Durban, and Stanger. He provided important information on each of them:

Kearsney—The first Sunday service was held on October 11, 1903. Rev. Rangiah preached from Zachariah 8:13. Mrs. Rangiah worked with her husband, providing leadership to the women. She visited them regularly, prayed for them, and provided care for the many who were sick. She also held special services where she taught women new songs, and led the Sunday School ministry at Kearsney.

---

14. Rangiah, *Reports*, 3.
15. Ibid.

Rangiah described a very significant meeting during which members discussed the ministry at Kearsney. Rev. D. Benjamin, Mr. Preyanadham, and Rev. and Mrs. Rangiah met to pray about the possibility of starting a church in Kearsney. The church there was organized on December 27, 1903. It was the first church of the Baptist Association of South Africa. Mr. D. Benjamin and K. Isaac were elected as deacons of this historic church.

Later, Rangiah baptized twelve and ended up with a membership of seventy-five. He composed hymns and choruses that he taught to the congregation. These songs gained popularity among the members of this church. Regular Sunday services, women's prayer, and prayer meetings were held. Once a month, the church held thanksgiving services; during these services new hymns and choruses were sung. A great sense of community characterized the services. Rangiah also held Bible studies during the summer vacation. Rev. D. Benjamin rendered great assistance to this church, especially when Rangiah was absent.

The church at Darnall was organized on May 22, 1904. The membership at Darnall was thirty-two, and it was reported that four people were baptized. According to Rangiah, this church was experiencing many challenges, details of which he does not mention.

The church in Stanger was organized in June 1904. There were six baptisms with a membership of thirty, including those who were baptized. Despite the challenge of having their house church removed by non-Christians, wrote Rangiah, this church was able to relocate to another area. Their members contributed financially and physically to the rebuilding of a house church. This building, which had a chapel, cost them six pounds, the equivalent of about $55 today.

The church in Durban was organized on December 25, 1904. There were no baptisms during that year. Its membership stood at fifteen. Rangiah reported that the school that had been established in Durban flourished. However, he was concerned about members relocating to other areas and attending other churches. Here, too, Rangiah expressed the need for revival in this church.

A LETTER TO THE EDITOR OF THE AMERICAN BAPTIST INTERNATIONAL MAGAZINE

Rangiah was concerned not only about the work in South Africa but globally as well. Evidence of this is found in his letter to an international

Baptist magazine in which he expressed concern for Indian mission in other parts of the world, including the United States. He wrote to the editor of the *American Baptist International Magazine*[16] about the need for missionaries to work with the Indian immigrants in San Francisco. He challenged Americans to consider learning the language of the Hindu immigrants so as to address their spiritual needs.

In concluding his report, Rangiah reflected on the work completed and the work still to be done. Clearly he was passionate about his work among the Telugus. He recognized that it was sustained by God, and he was keenly aware of the support he received from his wife.

He mentioned that both of them walked many miles visiting the Telugus in spreading the Gospel. Rangiah's report reflected a deep concern for the spiritual needs of the people. He did not dwell on the accomplishments he'd achieved by him in a short time, but pointed to the future and the task that was before him. He wrote that his most important work was to take care of the Christians and churches already formed. Secondly, it was to preach the Christian Gospel to those who had not yet received it.

Rangiah's letter to the editor provides insight into his knowledge of developments in global Baptist mission work. Paul Borthwick[17] contends that an important building block for world mission is reading, which was clearly among Rangiah's disciplines.

RANGIAH AND THE ABFMS'S DAVID DOWNIE

During Rangiah's work in South Africa, he made several invitations to the American Baptist Foreign Mission Society's Rev. David Downie and his wife to visit the Telugu Mission in South Africa. In the archives of the American Baptist Historical Society can be found a handwritten letter by John Rangiah to Rev. David Downie, an American Baptist missionary who played an important role in Rangiah's life while in Nellore, India. This letter contained some important context of Rangiah's work, including in the areas of human and financial resources as well as ministry needs.

Rangiah wrote about the status of the indentured laborers. He wrote that at the end of their contract, the majority of them "re-indentured" themselves while a few returned to India. He described the returning indentured laborers as common, uneducated, and shy. Rangiah advised

---

16. American Baptist Convention, 1911.
17. Borthwick, *Mind*, 67.

Downie, who was in India during this period, to make contact with the returning immigrants and inquire of them of the mission work in Natal. According to Rangiah, the uneducated and shy former laborers would provide a more accurate report of the work in South Africa than the educated indentured laborers. The reason for Rangiah's assumption is not known. It may be that Rangiah enjoyed more support from the uneducated laborers than from the educated ones. Later in his ministry, Rangiah experienced opposition from a segment of the indentured laborer community, which led to a split in the Indian Baptist work in South Africa.

The letter to Downie mentioned Palli Yellamanda and his wife, who served the Darnall Baptist Church, and Rev. D. Benjamin and his wife, who served in the Durban area. Rangiah stressed that since Durban was the chief port of the colony with a large Indian population, it required a church with a preacher. Rangiah wrote about his own position at Kearsney, the headquarters of the Baptist Association of South Africa, and the need for him to be based there. He also wrote about his many tours of other mission stations.

Rangiah made reference to the question, "How will the preachers for the work in Natal be paid?" He presented the cost for the support of a married preacher with a stipend of £1.10 per month and a single preacher with £1 per month, both with rations. Additionally, he stated that a preacher in Durban required £1 per month for rent.

In addition, Rangiah described how he raised support for those preachers. According to him, he stopped receiving support from the churches he planted. Instead he saved funds from these churches to support preachers. Rangiah reported that by June 11, 1905, he was able to save £20, with which he started a fund to support the preachers who were inducted and appointed by himself to the various mission stations in Natal. He mentioned that this amount would provide remuneration for five months. Rangiah was careful to indicate to the preachers that the fund would not provide support for them on a regular basis, as he felt that the church using their services was to meet that obligation. He encouraged the churches: "And in return the churches are exhorted to take heed to bear the burdens of our preachers, to their utmost possibility." He also wrote about the need to depend on God in this matter. In his letter, Rangiah expressed his appreciation for helpers who supported him in his ministry. He recorded that he was in prayer for three preachers, but received five. He compared them to the five talents referred to in the

Bible. According to Rangiah, two of the preachers—Colonel Addison of Stanger and W.G. Armstrong of Verulam—received remuneration from the estate owners.

A VISIT FROM FRIENDS

Rangiah considered the Downies his spiritual parents and longed for a visit from them. And on October 17, 1909, Downie and his wife landed in Durban, South Africa. Downie had much praise for Rangiah's work. He wrote:

> I knew something of the high opinion that Sir Liege Hulett (Rangiah's landlord) had of John and his work, but it was a surprise and a pleasure to hear from his own lips the very high regard he had for John and his work. Nor was Sir Liege the only one who spoke of it in similar terms. During our stay in Natal we heard nothing but the highest praise of his untiring work and Christ-like spirit. The work John has done is much more extensive than we had been led to believe from what he had written us.[18]

David Downie[19] wrote about his visit to South Africa at the invitation of John Rangiah: "It was a great delight to us to see the fine work John was doing . . . Sir Liege spoke in the highest of terms of John and his work." Downie's visit to South Africa helped in assessing the mission and the effectiveness of Rangiah's work among the Telugus. It is very evident from his comments that Downie was extremely pleased.

It appears that Downie had influenced Rangiah back in India. Rangiah wrote a personal letter to Downie and expressed his thanks for the role he played in his life in India. He then went on to report on his work in South Africa. In this handwritten letter, dated July 31, 1905, Rangiah addressed Downie as "My dearest Missionary father," an indication of the bond between the two. He wrote about the status of the indentured laborers who came from India to work on the sugar and tea estates. He also reported on the indentured labor system and its termination by the British government.

The termination of the indentured labor system by the British authorities in Natal meant that the flow of Indians to places like Kearsney, the hub of the Baptist Association of South Africa work, was stopped. To

---

18. Downie, *Lone Star*, 3.
19. Downie, *From the Mill to the Mission Field*, 53.

add to this Rangiah had to find resources to support the leaders he appointed over the churches in the Natal North Coast region. He reported to David Downie about assistance from local estate owners, Colonel Addison of Stanger and Mr. W. G. Armstrong, both of whom agreed to support preachers on their respective estates. Rangiah shared this blessing, and expressed thanks to God.

It was the first time in Rangiah's correspondence to the American Baptist Foreign Missionary Society that he raised the issue of finances. He did not raise it earlier because he maintained that the Indian church in South Africa should be self-supporting. So far, the Indian indentured laborers, out of their meager earnings, contributed to the work of the mission. Rangiah listed the number of preachers in service with the Telugu Mission in Natal. There were five, two of whom were supported by estate owners and three who were in need of support. The lack of funds did not impede the work among the Telugus. Some agreed to work without remuneration. Rev. Rangiah and his wife worked closely with these preachers to provide spiritual service to Telugu people.

Beginning in mid-1904, Rangiah made frequent visits to the South Coast, Isipingo, the Railway and Magazine barracks, and the Umgeni areas in Durban. He preached at evangelistic meetings to the many indentured laborers in these places, providing prayer and encouragement. He also sought permission from the Protector of Indian Immigrants to visit Indian passengers on the ships and in the immigration depot. In 1904, through Rangiah's vision and encouragement, a church was organized in Durban in the house of Mr. D. Benjamin. In 1909 this house church moved into a new building, which was dedicated and a foundation stone laid by Dr. David Downie. The work carried out by Rangiah received affirmation from another missionary to the Indians in the Natal province, Mr. N.E. Tomlinson of the South African General Mission (SAGM). This support of Rangiah's work is noteworthy given the general attitude of the dominant Baptist Union towards this indigenous mission work. Additionally, it was important for Rangiah that commendation from a person like Tomlinson be reported to the wider Christian community, as it provided a degree of objectivity.

3

John Rangiah's Theology and Model of Mission and Ministry

JOHN RANGIAH'S WORK AMONG the Indians was informed by a distinct theology that was influenced by American Baptist missionaries in India. He also demonstrated the ability to contextualize the Christian faith among the Indian Christians in South Africa.

The mission enterprise in South Africa in the 1800s saw European missionaries such as Andrew Murray, Jr., Johannes Van De Kemp, John Philip, and Robert Moffat of the London Missionary Society develop their own models for mission in South Africa. Rangiah, too, developed a model with unique characteristics.

In 1897, when the Christians in South India established the Telugu Home Missionary Society, they focused both on local and global mission, of which Rangiah was very much a part. Rangiah, like his American counterparts, recognized that mission must be to the farthest parts of the world, and he believed that Indians, irrespective of their ethnicity, country of origin, language, and social status, could participate in the missionary enterprise. Stan Nussbaum, in his attempt to clarify and simplify David Bosch's ideas and thoughts on mission,[1] wrote almost a century later about Luke's gospel with regards to mission and its universal appeal. Nussbaum states that the hearers in Luke's gospel, who appear to be Gentiles, were both the product of mission and the bearers of mission.

---

1. Nussbaum, *Guide*, 27.

Rangiah maintained that mission is universal in scope and is inseparably related to God's cosmic purposes.

The notion that mission was mainly carried out by the powerful western countries is negated by Rangiah, who represented a country that was poor and, at that time, a mission field. Additionally, his understanding of mission compares favorably with Bosch's understanding of mission with the exception of ethnicity, an issue to be discussed later. Bosch[2] states that mission should transcend class and ethnicity. Rangiah believed this and expressed it in his mission to South Africa.

Another significant insight into Rangiah's ministry was his view that women should be active participants in the ministry of the church. Rangiah's sterling report of the Women's Ministry reflected an understanding of ministry that encouraged the participation of women. He stated that his wife, Mrs. K. Rangiah, helped with the preaching of the gospel to the women. Her frequent visits to women made them very receptive to the gospel, and she enjoyed much success in her efforts to share the gospel. Mrs. Rangiah also taught at the school for children at Kearsney. As a result of this ministry, thirty-one new believers were added to the churches by baptism since 1904, reported Rangiah.[3]

In his mission report[4] Rangiah states that the American Baptist missionaries began their mission in India. They established many churches, primary schools, and high schools, as well as a college and two theological seminaries. Rangiah's mission efforts included the building of a school in Kearsney, as well as establishing churches in the then-Natal province.[5] His approach to mission embraced the notions that the social, educational, and spiritual needs of the Indian people are important. However, his work evidenced an emphasis on the educational and spiritual needs of the indentured laborers. (His approach to other race groups will be addressed later.)

Rangiah placed a strong emphasis on training local leaders for ministry. Although he did not advocate that the Telugus carry the Christian faith to other parts of the world, he trained laypersons to spread Christianity to many parts of Kwa Zulu Natal. He traveled the length and breadth of this province, preaching, teaching, and training persons for

---

2. Bosch, Introduction, 84–122.
3. Rangiah, *NIBA News*, 16.
4. Rangiah, *Reports*, 1.
5. Ibid., 4.

ministry. Among the lay leaders who received training for ministry were A. Reuben, D. Benjamin, V. Samson and Z. Robert.[6]

Rangiah adopted a very practical model for ministry among the Telugus. In his report he stated that in his missionary tours in South Africa, wherever he found groups of Christians, he gathered them into churches and appointed elders from among them. He challenged the elders to spread the gospel to the utmost parts to the best of their ability. In his report, he listed the churches that were established as a result of this model: the Verulam Church, established on May 22, 1904; the Darnall Church on June 12, 1904; the Durban Church on October 30, 1904; and the Stanger Church on December 25, 1904.

Having been schooled in India in theology, Rangiah was careful not to approach the South African mission from a purely Western perspective, which can sometimes be insensitive to the culture and customs of the local people. He communicated the gospel in terms understandable and appropriate to his audience. This was necessary as the Telugus were not very educated and had their own traditions and culture. As an evangelical, Rangiah took into account the cultural factors. Nicholls[7] in his book *Contextualization: A Theology of Gospel and Culture,* laments that evangelical communicators have often underestimated the importance of cultural factors in communication. Rangiah preached in the Telugu language and composed and taught Christian hymns to the Telugus. He and his wife organized activities such as Thanksgiving services, song festivals, and fellowship meetings, all of which were culturally oriented and spiritually relevant. They further assisted with planning weddings.

Rangiah organized and facilitated services that were culturally sensitive, that recognized the richness, diversity, and uniqueness of Indian culture—drama and theatre, music, and dance—as well as Indian ways of communicating. Rangiah and his wife composed hymns, poetry, and produced plays.

Although Rangiah received his theological training at an American Baptist seminary in India, he developed the ability to contextualize the Christian faith among the Telugus, unlike many Western missionaries who were sometimes culturally insensitive by teaching the local Christians to sing English hymns and play only the organ at church services. Rangiah

---

6. Rangiah, *NIBA News*, 15–22.
7. Nicholls, *Contextualization*, 9.

and his wife dressed like Indians. She wore her sari and he used his turban. But although Rangiah expressed the faith without disregarding the cultural practices among the Indian Baptists, his strategy did not take into account the social and political realities in Kwa Zulu Natal, a matter to be addressed later.

One striking feature of Rangiah's understanding of the Christian faith was his ecumenical outlook. The notion of relationship with other communions and bodies of believers was not only encouraged but was practiced by Rangiah himself. In 1910 Rangiah[8] sailed to Edinburgh, where he attended the International Missionary Conference, with all the leading denominations in attendance. The purpose of this international gathering of mission agencies was to promote unity in the missionary enterprise. According to the NIBA News,[9] Rangiah had an opportunity to speak at this conference, although there is no record of any public contribution by Rangiah.

Rangiah was one of five Asian delegates of the American Baptist Foreign Missionary Society. Stanley makes the point that Rangiah was not simply the first missionary sent by the Telugu Baptist Home Missionary Society to the Telugu-speaking Christians of the sugar plantations in Natal, but he was also the first overseas missionary sent by any of the mission churches of the American Baptists. Stanley further observes that Rangiah is an early example of what would be called a "south to south" mission.[10]

Writing about his impressions of the conference, Rangiah commented on the global scope of the gathering. He was also impressed with the cleanliness of Edinburgh, surprised at the absence of idols, and grateful for the benevolence of his hosts. He wrote that he was motivated by his experience in Edinburgh and eager to return to South Africa with a greater determination to engage in ministry.[11]

THE IMPACT OF THE BIBLE ON RANGIAH'S MINISTRY

The formation of theology does not occur in a vacuum, but is influenced by a number of factors, including context, culture, and education. Rangiah lived most of his adult life in India. He received his education

---

8. Rangiah, *NIBA News*, 25.
9. Ibid.
10. Stanley, *Conference*, 100.
11. Rangiah, *Missions*, 662–63.

there and followed Indian culture, which was therefore deeply rooted in his psyche but at the same time conflicted with the Christian faith, as expressed by the American Baptist missionaries during Rangiah's stay in India. It is against this background that one must attempt to analyze Rangiah's theology.

As mentioned earlier, Rangiah's early years were spent with American Baptists in the country of his birth, India. These American Baptist missionaries were part of a strong denomination that had its evangelical roots in England. Rangiah was schooled in evangelical theology in India at a school started by American Baptist missionaries. By and large, he employed this theology in his work in South Africa. His understanding and interpretation of the Bible must be seen against his early association with and schooling in an American Baptist theological institution.

American Baptists have a distinct denominational identity. They are a biblically based people whose life and witness are grounded in the Scriptures. Broadly, American Baptist missionaries' theology centered on God's sovereignty in which the theology of the Kingdom and the church feature strongly. Furthermore, according to this theology, Baptists are biblically based, inclusive, redeemed, interdependent, missional, and worshipping in character.[12] This theological orientation became very evident in Rangiah's work in South Africa. Rangiah can be best described as a moderate evangelical who sometimes leaned towards a conservative orientation.

Roger Olson[13] lists the core characteristics of authentic evangelical theology as follows: (1) the Bible is the supreme norm of truth for Christian belief and practices and that the Biblical message is enshrined in its interpretation of those narratives; (2) a supernatural worldview that is centered in a transcendent personal God who interacts with and intervenes in creation; (3) the forgiving and transforming grace of God through Jesus Christ in the experience called conversion. This experience is the center of authentic Christian experience; (4) the primary task of Christian theology is to serve the Christian Church's mission of bringing God's grace to the whole world through proclamation and service.

Rangiah worked out of this evangelical paradigm. However, there are features within his evangelical theology that place him more on the conservative side theologically. For instance, except for the establishment

---

12. Simmons, "Inquiry."
13. Olson, "Does Evangelical Theology Have a Future?" 40.

of a school for the Telugu children in Kearsney, he concentrated largely on evangelism and very little on social issues. This stands in contrast to contemporary evangelicals such as Ron Sider,[14] who asserts that Christian ministry should address both evangelism and social engagement. Sider[15] quotes Alan Walker: "There is no greater menace than a born-again Christian without a social conscience."

In preparing leaders and congregants, Rangiah believed that the Bible was critical in shaping their lives. He held Bible classes at Kearsney where he chose the lives of Bible characters such as Joseph, Samson, and Ruth as models for the male and female leaders and congregants.[16]

Rangiah's dependence on God evidenced a belief in the supernatural. In coming to South Africa as a missionary, he realized that no human effort would convince his wife to agree to accompany him on such a mission. He engaged in prayer, which yielded the desired result. He commented, "God worked wonders."[17] He also believed that when he first arrived in Kearsney and was in need of accommodation, it was God's intervention that resulted in Sir James Hulett's providing it. As noted earlier, his prayer was, "He raiseth up the poor out of the dust and lifteth the needy out of the dunghill."[18]

Rangiah championed the Bible as the bedrock of his Christian life and practice, as evidenced by his letterhead, dated 1905. On the letterhead is the name of the mission, Telugu Baptist, followed by his name, Rev. John Rangiah. The address on the letterhead is Kearsney, South Africa, and it features a drawing of a dove carrying a branch with the biblical text of Isaiah 61:1 written below:

> The Spirit of the Lord God is upon me; because the Lord hath anointed me to preach good tidings unto the meek; he hath sent me to bind up the broken-hearted, to proclaim liberty to the captives, and the opening of the prison to them that are bound; To proclaim the acceptable year of the Lord, and the day of vengeance of our God; to comfort all that mourn; To appoint unto them that mourn in Zion, to give unto them beauty for ashes, the oil of joy for mourning, the garment of praise for the spirit of heaviness;

14. Sider, *Scandal*, 121–35.
15. Sider, *Scandal*, 136.
16. Rangiah, *NIBA News*, 18.
17. Ibid., 10.
18. Ibid., 13.

that they might be called trees of righteousness, the planting of the Lord, that he might be glorified.

This text provides an insight into Rangiah's faith. It seems to convey the idea that God has found favor in him and has put the Holy Spirit upon him as a seal of approval for the task of mission. Rangiah understood his task to be that of a missionary who engaged in extensive preaching.

Rangiah took his ministry to the broken-hearted very seriously. His very first experience was of a Telugu man who was found guilty of murdering a fellow Indian. This criminal was awaiting execution when Rangiah was informed about his fate. Rangiah provided spiritual support for him and even pleaded with the Governor of Natal to spare the man's life, but he was unsuccessful.[19]

After the condemned man responded favorably to Rangiah's counsel and indicated that he was ready to accept the Christian faith, Rangiah read a text from 2 Corinthians 4:7: "But we have this treasure in earthen vessels, that the excellency of the power may be of God, and not of us." It appears that Rangiah was encouraging the condemned man to understand that his body was merely a fragile container that held his soul. Before the execution, the man gave a speech in which he repented of his crime and described how the Christian faith had transformed his life.[20]

Another line in the text found of Rangiah's letterhead also provides insight into his passion for his fellow Telugus. It reads, " . . . to proclaim liberty to the captives, and the opening of the prison to them that are bound." Clearly, he believed that many of the Telugus were in need of spiritual freedom.

From the time of his arrival in South Africa Rangiah was an avid reader of the Bible. It is recorded that when the ship on which he was traveling from India to Durban, the *Safari*, docked at 6 p.m. at the Durban harbor, the passengers had to remain on board overnight until the next morning before disembarking. During this time Rangiah read the Bible, in particular the Acts of the Apostles.[21] In concluding his report of the Telugu Baptist Mission to the Telugu Baptist Home Missionary Society, Rangiah quoted[22] a very significant biblical text from Malachi 3:10–12,

---

19. Ibid., 12.
20. Ibid.
21. Ibid., 11.
22. Rangiah, *Reports*, 5.

"All nations shall call you blessed; for ye shall be a delightsome land, saith the Lord of Hosts."

It is not easy to clearly define Rangiah's theological orientation based on his ministry in South Africa because the Indian Baptist church did not label people based on theological persuasion. Furthermore, the vast majority of the indentured laborers were illiterate.[23] However, since Rangiah's theological educational background was influenced by American Baptists, he worked mainly out of their paradigm, which emphasized the sovereignty of God, the kingdom of God, and the church. There is much debate in Christendom about the sovereignty of God regarding salvation. Both Calvinist and Arminian views take into account the sovereignty of God, but there is divergence with regard to defining the sovereignty of God pertaining to salvation. For Calvinists, the sovereignty of God is a cardinal aspect of their understanding of salvation. According to this understanding,[24] God has the right to elect one person to be saved and to reprobate another. The Arminian view maintains that humanity has a free will with regard to their salvation.

Rangiah's approach to salvation reflects an Arminian orientation. As noted above, his first ministry assignment was to a prisoner named Subbadoo. Rangiah feared that Subbadoo would harden his heart towards God but was later pleased that Subbadoo made a decision to accept the Christian faith.[25] In the twelve years Rangiah worked in Natal, his hymns[26] featured the theme of salvation. In evangelistic services, he reported persons making decisions to receive salvation.[27]

The adventurous spirit and trusting faith of men like Paul the apostle became evident in Rangiah's life and ministry. Like Paul, Rangiah traveled on missionary assignments, planting churches and training and mentoring leaders for ministry.

THE PRIORITY OF PRAYER

Rangiah believed and maintained that prayer was an important spiritual discipline and practice. Prayer was featured prominently in his reports.

23. Rangiah, *NIBA News*, 16.
24. Birch, "Sovereignty and Rule," 1.
25. Rangiah, *NIBA News*, 12.
26. Rangiah, *Teluga Mission*, 1.
27. Rangiah, *NIBA News*, 17–27.

In 1902, when Rangiah was initially challenged to go to South Africa to work among the Telugu Christians, he went to his knees and prayed for God's will to be done.[28] It was a simple act of submission to God. Indeed, prayer and submission to God were hallmarks of his work as a missionary.

Rangiah's writings emphasize both prayer and self sufficiency. In preparing for his ministry in South Africa, he spent three months in prayer.[29] When his wife resisted the idea of their going to Natal, Rangiah spent time in fasting and prayer. His prayer was:

O Lord grant if it is thy will that we should labor in Natal for Thee, open Thou the way. Grant Kanakamma courage, O lord, that she may be able to leave her beloved parents and friends and undertake the journey with me. Do tell us, O Lord, whether to leave behind these my two children or to take them with me. If it is Thy will that we leave them behind, grant Kanakamma and me that courage to endure the pangs of separation. Help us on our voyage and use us for Thy glory and service.[30]

This prayer reflected a person's deep concern for his family and ministry. Rangiah recognized the spiritual resource that is available to Christians, particularly as indicated in Proverbs 3:6: "Commit to the Lord whatever you do, and your plans will succeed." This text suggests an understanding of the supremacy of God in matters of family and ministry and that God must direct these matters. Rangiah's prayer was answered within six weeks. His wife informed him that she was ready to go to Natal and that there should be no delay.[31]

In 1903, when Rangiah arrived at Port Natal, he was so overwhelmed by the task before him that he prayed for God's strength and grace. When he arrived in Kearsney, he organized a prayer meeting for the sole purpose of establishing a church there. The result was the forming of the first Telugu Baptist Church in Africa.[32]

In Natal, prayer continued to feature strongly in Rangiah's ministry. In 1906, he prayed for the outpouring of the Holy Spirit. He maintained that prayer was necessary for personal cleansing. At a prayer meeting in 1906, congregants wept and cried aloud as they prayed for mercy and

---

28. Ibid., 8.
29. Ibid.
30. Ibid., 9.
31. Ibid., 10.
32. Ibid., 11–14.

forgiveness. It was reported that these prayer meetings were held over a period of four months. In Nonoti, a hill (which was named Prayer Hill) was a place Rangiah and others went to pray. Rangiah also initiated home prayer meetings.[33]

Rangiah wrote that he and his wife prayed earnestly for buildings and for places of worship, and he gave thanks to God for providing them in places like Stanger and Verulam. In his second and third reports he lists the number of pastors he appointed to the churches and the churches' financial support of those pastors despite their economic status. He wrote, "We are trying hard to help ourselves, and when we do our part, we know the Lord will care for the rest."

Rangiah recognized the impact of prayer with regard to education for the Telugus. He established a school in Kearsney. Here American Baptists in India influenced his theology on education. American Baptists, according to R. H. Elliot et al.[34] held to the view that the "whole context of our humanity, therefore, is involved in our mission." In their work in India, American Baptist missionaries shared the Christian faith with the Telugus and contributed to the educational advancement and social uplifting of these people by building schools and hospitals. The NIBA News[35] recorded that, as a missionary, Rangiah was responsible not only for the spiritual needs of the Indians in Natal, but also for the educational requirements of the many Indian children who were growing up illiterate. He once again presented this need to God in prayer. It is recorded that he went down on his knees and asked for God's guidance and help. In answer to his prayer, his landlords, the Huletts, provided an old laundry building. On Monday, October 10, 1904, the first Indian school in Kearsney opened, with four pupils in attendance. By the end of the year, enrollment increased to twelve.[36]

EMPHASIZING SALVATION

It seems from Rangiah's letterhead that his call to South Africa was based on the Isaiah 61:1 text. Although it is difficult to base one's theology on this text—such a text without exegesis is insufficient to do any meaningful

---

33. Ibid., 17–21.
34. Elliot, "American Baptist."
35. Rangiah, *NIBA News*, 16.
36. Ibid.

analysis—it nevertheless conveys the idea that Rangiah was driven by this call to preach salvation.

Furthermore, Rangiah's hymn entitled *New Birth*[37] reflects this theme of salvation. The English translation[38] is:

New Birth

Chorus

The great teacher Jesus Christ confirmed that man should be born again in order to enter into heaven. Nicodemus the leader of the Jews who knew the law was thinking of Jesus He went at night to the Lord, stood before him and talks to him in peace. Rabbi, you are teaching about the word of the Lord of heaven and we understand it. And the signs (works) of God that you do, cannot be done by ungodly men. As the Pharisees said these things Jesus replied to him with grace and mercy. Jesus told him the truth that none can be lifted up to the Kingdom of heaven without the new birth. The Pharisees asked how an old man can enter his mother's womb to be born again. Then Jesus said unless you are born of the spirit you cannot enter into the Kingdom of God.

Rangiah's hymn is based on John 3:1–21. In Protestant Christianity salvation is understood to be grounded in the life, death, and resurrection of Jesus Christ. The result of the death, burial, and resurrection of Christ is redemption.[39] It is at this point that a person experiences new life. Many instances in Rangiah's ministry reflected aspects of salvation. As previously noted, his first ministry opportunity was a visit to a prisoner, resulting in the prisoner's salvation.[40] It appears that Rangiah believed in the universal saving will of God and that salvation is possible only in and through Christ. Rangiah invited the prisoner in Durban to choose to either accept or reject salvation. He chose salvation.[41]

---

37. 1890.
38. Ramanjulu, letter to author, January 2010.
39. McGrath, *Christian Theology*, 407.
40. Rangiah, *Reports*, 1.
41. Ibid.

ESCHATOLOGICAL HOPE

Rangiah, in a hymn titled *The Door to Heaven*,[42] wrote about the hope. The English translation[43] of this hymn is as follows:

Christ is the Door of Heaven

Chorus

> Jesus is the beautiful door-the beautiful door-on the way to heaven. He is the beautiful door through which you enter into the land of Canaan where the milk and honey flow. He is the beautiful door through which people enter into the Holy place of the temple in Jerusalem. He is the beautiful door through which we enter into heaven as the priest of the holy of the holiest. He is the beautiful door which is the right door even though it is narrow, it leads us to happiness in spite of troubles.

This hymn reflects Johannine imagery and eschatology, which constitutes, at the very least, standard evangelical theology.[44] Eschatology in the Christian tradition comes from the Greek term *ta eschata* ("the last things") and relates to such matters as the Christian expectations of Christ's resurrection and judgment.[45] It appears that Rangiah, through this hymn, was presenting hope to the indentured laborers in the midst of suffering. It must be stated that it is precarious to extrapolate from Rangiah's hymn any meaning without an understanding of his social context.[46] We do know through the writings of Dhupelia-Mesthrie[47] that indentured laborers suffered. There is no record of Rangiah addressing these sufferings, though he does, through this hymn (although written in 1890) provide hope to the indentured laborers who were suffering.

---

42. 1890.
43. Ramanjulu, letter.
44. Craig Keener, interview with author, Palmer Theological Seminary, 2010.
45. McGrath, *Christian Theology*, 553.
46. Keener, interview.
47. Dhupelia-Mesthrie, *From Fields to Freedom*.

RANGIAH'S RESPONSE TO SOCIO-POLITICAL CONDITIONS IN SOUTH AFRICA

Racial tension began very early in the history of South Africa. De Gruchy[48] argued that this racism, which in 1948 became known as apartheid, began as early as 1910. As a result, Baptists were segregated along racial lines. The Telugu Baptists functioned as an ethnic church. And even if they wanted to embrace other racial groups, the conditions in South Africa would not have allowed it. Additionally, the missionaries—Methodists, German and Norwegian Lutherans, the French Oblates of Mary Immaculate, the Anglicans, Scottish Presbyterians, and members of the American Board of Missions—began their work in a highly segregated context. When integration did take place, Africans were generally ostracized by their own people and discriminated against by the white community. Isichei[49] records what an African Methodist said in 1863: "To the natives we are despised—to the English we are no more than Kaffirs." Indians suffered the same fate as Blacks, albeit not as severely.

Rangiah lived in British-controlled India until he left for South Africa. Since the seventeenth century, India had been influenced by British politics and social life, thus Rangiah was accustomed to British rule in Natal. His relationship with the English in Natal, including with his landlord Sir Liege Hullett and others, demonstrated his ability to approach them regarding his work among the Indians. However, Rangiah had no need to confront them on issues of discrimination and injustices that Indians experienced, as the records in BASA history do not show any discrimination and injustices by the Hulletts against the indentured Indians.

Rangiah's theological orientation did not allow him to address such social and political issues. Theologically he was schooled in India by American Baptist missionaries. American Baptist theology at that time did not challenge socio-political injustices in India. Advocates of this theology were mainly white males who did not strongly address social issues. American missionaries addressed these issues through socially oriented ministries such as the building of schools, hospitals, and colleges for the low caste Telugus in India.

In India, Rangiah appreciated these positive contributions of American Baptist missionaries This approach to ministry influenced his

---

48. De Gruchy, *Struggle*, 53.
49. Isichei, *History*, 100.

work in South Africa. The American missionaries in India did not confront the British authorities' unfair treatment of the Telugus. It seemed that Rangiah, as a result of his years in British-controlled India, was accustomed to such a political system and therefore did not find it difficult to adapt to such a system in Natal. It appears that he did not believe he had the right as a foreigner to confront the British in Natal over any injustice or discrimination. In this regard it would be unfair to criticize the American Baptist missionaries in India for not doing the same.

JOHN RANGIAH'S LEGACY

When the Rangiahs left India for South Africa, they did so with the understanding that the church in South Africa would provide most of their remuneration. Since they were deeply committed to prayer, they further believed that God would take care of their needs. The Hullets, at Kearsney, were touched by their humility and love for God and of their own will provided a stipend of £20 per annum for the Rangiahs, reinforcing the Rangiahs' belief in prayer. When finances became an issue during the tension between Rangiah and some in the congregation who accused him of living a sumptuous lifestyle, he requested that the contribution by the church in India be stopped. He also believed that the church in South Africa should take responsibility for providing for its physical needs—further evidence of his life of faith and integrity.

What is of great significance as one considers missions in Third World countries is the tendency of nationals to be dependent on overseas financial support. While this is needed for a period of time, there must come a time when the nationals need to become less dependent on Western support and become more self-sufficient. Rangiah shows this very clearly in his mission among the Telugus. He went one step further by stating that the sending mission agency in India, the Telugu Home Mission Society, should bear the responsibility of sustaining the work among the Telugus in South Africa, but that this work should be carried out and supported by the Indians in South Africa.[50]

The training of Telugu lay leaders for ministry was a hallmark of Rangiah's work. Having received education himself in India, he recognized its importance and set out to educate his parishioners. He built a school in Kearsney, trained men and women to lead congregations, and

---

50. Rangiah, *Reports*, 1–5.

appointed regional representatives to take care of the spiritual needs of the congregations. Given the lack of educational opportunities for Indians in the early 1900s in South Africa, Rangiah stands out as an important pioneer in the education of the Telugus in South Africa. Out of the school he established came many men and women who have contributed to the advancement of the Indian population in South Africa.

Rangiah's arrival as an indigenous missionary to South Africa must be hailed as a great milestone, since at that time mostly western missionaries went to Third World countries. Furthermore, he negated the idea that only western missionaries were capable of undertaking such an enterprise. Peruvian-born missiologist Samuel Escobar[51] stated in his book *The New Global Missions: The Gospel from Everywhere to Everyone,* that the Great Commission is directed not only to Western Christians but to everyone. Rangiah showed that as a Third World Christian, he was capable of participating in global missions. He did not allow his ethnicity, economic status, and country of origin to impede his call to South Africa, and he did this over 100 years ago.

Although Rangiah demonstrated that as a Third World missionary he could participate in global missions, he did not intentionally stress the need for South African Indians to consider foreign mission work. Somehow the missionary spirit of Rangiah did not influence Baptist Indians in South Africa to the extent that it would become a sending agent, though such an emphasis would come later. Rangiah did encourage local missions, but this was confined to Indians in South Africa. It seems that the failure of Rangiah to engender a missionary spirit and zeal among the Indians in South Africa was due partly to the fact that the Telugu population was in need of so much training. Much work was needed to strengthen and prepare them for such a task. After all, these people were indentured laborers, and their only medium of language was Telugu. Since India was the only country that had a Telugu-speaking population, the door for foreign missions for Telugus in the 1900s was limited.

Another observation in Rangiah's work is that nowhere in the records of the history of the BASA is there reference to any relationship with Black Christian leaders or congregations. It may be because of the 1906 African uprising, which took place because of a poll tax that the white authorities were enforcing on Zulu males in Natal. This uprising

---

51. Escobar, *Missions*, 12.

caused Rangiah to be fearful of being attacked. According to The NIBA News, Rangiah wrote[52] that the uprising caused great alarm and confusion. The indentured laborers were stricken with fear and took shelter in the tea factory during the night in fear for their lives. Rangiah and his family spent many nights hiding in the bushes at Gospel Hill at Kearsney. Another factor could have been the language barrier. While Rangiah was very proficient in English, he could not really use this language to minister to the Zulus.

Perhaps the greatest historical significance of the arrival of the Rangiahs in South Africa was their establishment of the BASA, whose work was not a product of colonial missions work as is the case with White, Colored and Black Baptist work in South Africa. Baptist organizations from these racial populations fell under the jurisdiction of the Baptist Union of South Africa, a largely English denomination. The BASA work stands out as the most unique mission in South Africa because it was started by an Indian-born missionary and was and is an autonomous organization with its own constitution and structure.

The sugar and tea industries in South Africa benefited greatly from the contributions of the indentured laborers. Not only did these two industries gain from their labor, but these laborers added richly to the culture and economy of Natal. Today one of the greatest concentrations of Indians outside of India is in Phoenix and Chatsworth, South Africa. These two Townships were BASA mission fields. The results of hard work by BASA pioneers are also evident in Phoenix and Chatsworth.

We turn our attention now to others—including John Rangiah's son, Theophilius, who followed John Rangiah from India to South Africa.

---

52. Rangiah, *NIBA News*, 17.

4

Following in John Rangiah's Footsteps

THE STRAIN OF PROVIDING leadership to such a vast area from Durban to Kearsney in the Natal North Coast was taking its toll on the Rangiahs. At the suggestion of Dr. Downie, additional personnel were brought from India to assist with the Telugu work.

REINFORCING THE TELUGU BAPTIST MISSION: REV. V. C. JACOB

The arrival of Rev. Valpula C. Jacob in 1910 to serve as the second missionary from India inaugurated a new era in the history of the Indian Baptists. Rev. Jacob, a teacher for a number of years in the Ramapatnam Theological Seminary, felt the call to come to South Africa to work among the Telugus. The Jacobs were welcomed by Rev. Rangiah and others at the Durban docks and received warmly by the Telugus in South Africa.

Both Jacob and Rangiah worked well among the Telugus. On April 21, 1911 Jacob was invited to live in Durban and to provide spiritual care for the members of Somseu Road Baptist Church. Jacob worked with Rev. Rangiah, visiting various churches, preaching, counseling and encouraging the Telugu population. He spent three months in Kearsney at the home of the Rangiahs. In July of 1912, Jacob left South Africa and returned to India due to ill health. He was described as being highly regarded by his peers in India as well as by the missionaries of the ABFMS. He handed all the records of the mission to John Rangiah. However, he returned on December 13, 1915 to continue work as a missionary in South Africa.

Jacob served until his death in 1932. He was an outstanding leader who worked well among the Telugus in Natal.[1]

THEOPHILIUS M. RANGIAH

Rev. Theophilius M. Rangiah, the eldest son of John and Kanakamma Rangiah, arrived in South Africa from India in 1903 with his parents when he was six years old. At age 10, he returned to India for further schooling. He received his early education at the school that had been established by his parents in Kearsney. He attended the Coles-Ackerman Memorial Boys' High School in Nellore, India. In India, Theophilius was brought up in the strictest and most orthodox environment under the care of his maternal grandmother. After completing high school, he studied at the Madras Christian College of the University of Madras in preparation for becoming a lawyer. During his second year as an Arts degree student, Theophilius was invited to Natal, South Africa to work among the Telugus. Before arriving in South Africa, he married Sugunamma Narsiah.[2]

In 1921 Rev. Theophilius Rangiah and Sugunamma arrived in Kearsney. He continued in the work his mother and father had started among the Indians, focusing on re-organization and church planting. Theophilius began by visiting the churches that had been established by his parents. He acquainted himself with the people and the state of every area where BASA churches were located. He also made contact with the white landlords and managers of the indentured laborers, encouraging them to take an interest in the spiritual needs of their employees. He encouraged indentured laborers to consecrate their lives and to maintain holy living. He believed that a close relationship with God was a prerequisite for evangelism. In order to accomplish this, he held Consecration Meetings for pastors, deacons, evangelists, and other office bearers of the BASA Church. He further stressed that these men and women would attain true leadership not by virtue of their knowledge, prestige, and influence but rather by their Christ-like lives.

Under his leadership, a number of churches were established and grew. At Glendale, Theophilius began ministry among the Indian laborers who worked at the Glendale Sugar Estate. The result was the establishment of the Glendale Baptist Church on December 16, 1923. His

---

1. Jacob and Cornelius, *Brochure*, 23.
2. Israel, *History*, 4.

leadership contributed to the growth of the Darnall Baptist Church. The first building of this church was made of grass. A wood and iron building replaced the grass building, and then another building was constructed to accommodate the numerical growth of this church.

Theophilius was responsible for the establishment of the Umhlali Baptist Church on October 14, 1923. In Durban, a church was established in Cato Manor; it later relocated to Hillary. Theophilius visited all these churches. He also raised funds to purchase property in North Street, Durban, where a church was built to accommodate the congregation in the Durban area.

Despite the BASA schism in 1914, the two Baptist organizations cooperated with each other. Theophilius assisted the Baptist Mission with its need for a missionary. A request was made to the Telugu Home Mission Society in India to send a missionary to South Africa. Rev. V.J. Jacob responded, arriving in Durban on July 28, 1936. In Durban, he and his wife worked with the Baptist Mission churches.

Theophilius Rangiah expanded the work of his parents that had begun in 1903. He died in 1947 after serving as a missionary for almost twenty-six years. After his death, European Baptists[3] assisted the Indians to continue with the BASA work.

The work of the Rangiahs, which started off as a Telugu church, became an inclusive church of which Tamil-speaking and Hindi-speaking people became a part. However, Timothy Paul in his thesis makes certain claims about the Rangiahs' attitude towards the Tamilians. Paul, a Tamilian,[4] asserts that Tamil Baptists were sidelined by Telugu Baptists with regard to leadership positions. It seems there was a manifestation of the caste system among the Baptist Indians in Natal. The indentured Baptist Indians, who were mainly from the south of India, spoke primarily Telugu. While a few spoke Tamil, all worshiped in a predominantly Telugu-speaking church in Natal.[5]

REV. D. N. NATHANIEL

After the death of Theophilius Rangiah in 1947, the Indian Baptist Church was without a missionary until 1951, when Rev. David Newton

---

3. Ibid., 10.
4. Paul, "From Church to Church," 144.
5. (NIBA News 1953: 8)

Nathaniel and his family arrived in Natal on the ship *Isipingo* to take up the position of superintendent missionary. Nathaniel was born on October 24, 1908 in the district of Ramayapatnam in South India.[6] Prior to his arrival, he was ordained in Allur, India after completing theological studies at the Ramapatnum Theological Seminary, an American Baptist seminary where he trained as a minister, as well as at the Bangalore Theological College in India, supported by the Baptist Mission of England. Nathaniel's early education was in a mission school in Kavali, India. He was married to Jayamma.

To commemorate Nathaniel, N. Timothy, a former general secretary of the BASA, wrote a biography of Nathaniel wherein he records the tributes paid by the churches in India to Nathaniel just before he left for South Africa. These included tributes by the field association, which comprised eleven churches; the Southern Baptist Association; the Lone Star Baptist Church (the church that John Rangiah had been a member of); and other churches. The Telugu Baptist Church in Allur wrote "Your meritorious services to the Church as deacon, secretary, treasurer and Sunday School Superintendent have always been helpful to the growth of the church."[7]

There were also warnings by some in India about Nathaniel's going to South Africa. In a letter dated September 30, 1950, Nathaniel's call to South Africa was questioned, as there was a delay of almost a year before Nathaniel finally left India for South Africa. The letter stated "If you go to South Africa you and your whole family will be beheaded the moment you step out of the boat. If you want to go, go yourself, but leave your family here." Nathaniel replied, "We must serve the Lord not only when all things go well but even under adverse circumstances."[8]

On June 9, 1951 the Nathaniels arrived with their three children to work among the Telugus. They were received warmly by the Natal Indian Baptist Association. At a reception in Durban, the missionary and his family were treated to a welcome service.

> You, represent Sir, a rare combination of two important factors which are so very necessary in the ministry of our churches in this country, since we have in you a harmonious blend of high

---

6. Timothy, *Diamond Jubilee*, 7.
7. Timothy, *Silver Jubilee*, 4.
8. Ibid., 5–6.

academic qualifications and practical experience accumulated over a number of years.[9]

It seemed when Nathaniel indicated to the churches in India his intention to go to South Africa as a missionary, there were those who were not supportive and who ridiculed him at times. One church leader stated, "This is of your own choice and a capricious thinking." It seemed that Nathaniel not only faced this kind of reaction from a few leaders in India, but also from others during his work as a missionary in South Africa. In fact some in the BASA ridiculed and mentally abused him.[10]

Despite this, Nathaniel served the BASA churches as a superintendent missionary for almost thirty-five years, working hard and faithfully among the Telugus. He became the superintendent missionary of NIBA in 1951. He wrote many Telugu songs and translated some popular hymns into Telugu. The staff of the South African Baptist Missionary Society (SABMS), a body formed by the Baptist Union, visited the Indian churches regularly. Rev. T. D. Pass of the Baptist Union worked closely with Rev. Nathaniel. Pass introduced Nathaniel to the circuit system, in which a minister pastored several churches in a particular region.[11]

All of the missionaries who came from India stressed the value of education. All received quality education from the American Baptist Foreign Missionary Society's educational program in India. This is evident in the missionaries' attitude toward theological education. Nathaniel is no exception. He gained his Master of Divinity degree at the age of seventy at the University of Durban Westville in Durban. He had completed the degree of Bachelor of Divinity and arrived in Natal with a good theological education.[12] Dr. P. M. Krishna, a warden at the Bethesda Bible College in Durban, sponsored Nathaniel's theological graduate studies and also promised to do so himself until he completes the Doctor of Divinity.[13]

In the early years of Nathaniel's work as a missionary with the BASA, Nathaniel wrote about unification and the need to work closely with the other Indian Baptists. In his thesis, he presents a strong theological basis

---

9. Ibid., 7.
10. Ibid., 10.
11. Israel, *History*, 4.
12. Timothy, *Diamond Jubilee*, 7.
13. Timothy, *Silver Jubilee*, 16.

for unity and cooperation among the Telugus in South Africa.[14] He states, "To this end no stone should be left unturned, unity then must be advocated and encouraged by every member and by every church."

As a theologically trained minister, Rev. Nathaniel stimulated the thinking of the Indians with regard to ministry. He wrote several books and commentaries: *Helpful Commentary on Phillipians, For the Preacher in the Making, Simple talks on Christian Doctrines, Three minute Digest, Commentaries on Deuteronomy* and *Pastoral Epistle*.[15] He died at the age of seventy-seven on December 20, 1985.

---

14. Nathaniel, *Origin and Development*.
15. Timothy, *Silver Jubilee*, 1–16.

5

Schism in the Indian Baptist Church

THE BAPTIST ASSOCIATION OF South Africa church that was pioneered by Rangiah was not without challenges. Tensions arose between Rangiah and certain members of the Kearsney Baptist Church. This led to a schism. Rangiah[1] wrote, "The year 1913 was an unpleasant one for the Mission, for differences arose between the Missionary, Rev. John Rangiah, and a certain section of his congregation." Rangiah preached a sermon on the subject of sin and its results. A certain section of the congregation viewed his preaching on this subject as controversial, and interpreted it as their excommunication from the congregation.

These aggrieved members took this matter up with the Telugu Baptist Home Missionary Society (TBHMS) in India. They sent a letter without the knowledge of Rangiah to the TBHMS. Rangiah was disappointed that he was not informed about the letter. The TBHMS responded by sending a representative to South Africa to attend to this conflict.

Rev. W. B. Boggs represented the TBHMS. On May 31, 1914, a council of sixty-six members met at Kearsney and deliberated over the conflict for twenty-four hours. Despite the intervention of Rev. Boggs, the talks failed. Rev. Rangiah resigned.[2]

The Baptist Missionary Review, a publication of the American Baptist Church USA, records[3] this schism. Unfortunately it does not provide reasons, but states that Rangiah was not acceptable to a considerable number

1. Rangiah *NIBA News*, 8–10.
2. Ibid., 10.
3. Marsh, *Review*, 381.

of the Telugu Baptists in Natal. However, churches that were established by Rangiah,[4] such as the Verulam Church (1904), The Darnall Church (1904), The Durban Church (1904), and the Stanger Church (1904), remained under Rangiah's ministry, thus it seems only a small segment of the Telugus in Natal did not accept Rangiah. To date, there has been no information about the actual cause of the schism.

According to the Golden Jubilee Brochure, a publication of the aggrieved group, the two parties, headed by Rangiah on one side and Mr. Y. A. Lazarus on the other, were unwilling to compromise. On December 27, 1914, Rangiah formed the Natal Baptist Association of South Africa, now called the Baptist Association of South Africa. The other group called itself the Indian Baptist Mission and is now the Baptist Mission of South Africa. Despite this setback, Rangiah went on to build the BASA into a viable Baptist organization centered mainly in the Kwa Zulu Natal province. After many years of faithful service, Rangiah died on December 23, 1915. He was deeply missed because of the significant leadership he gave to the Telugus, especially those on the North Coast of Durban.

It is important to examine Paul's assertions on the relationship between the Tamil and Telugu Baptists as well as the comments of individuals on the reasons for the previously mentioned split between John Rangiah's group and the aggrieved group led by Y. A. Lazarus. In this split, it is alleged by some individuals that Tamil-speaking congregants were discriminated against by the Telugu-speaking leaders. This social categorization requires some additional background because of its implications for the Indian Baptist Church in Natal.

Within the Indian Baptist community were members of the Mala and the Madiga people. John Rangiah, a Telugu, belonged to the Mala (sometimes spelled Malla) group. The Tamil speaking Baptists belonged to the Madigas. These two formed part of a social group called the untouchables or Dalits. The untouchables came mainly from Andra Pradesh; they were marginalized in every respect by those higher up in the caste system. The untouchables fell outside of the caste system, which meant that they were outcasts who lived away from the higher castes. Their lives were shaped

---

4. Rangiah *NIBA News*, 15.

by a system of sanctified apartheid.[5] The hierarchal caste system comprised the Brahmans, Kshatriya, Vaishya, and Shudra.[6]

Within the untouchable social groups, the Malas, Madigas and Dakkals were divided by heredity.[7] Language also divided the untouchables. The untouchables applied the same social rules of endogamy of the caste system. Members of these social systems married exclusively within the caste or sub-caste system.[8]

Some held to the view that the 1911 Indian Baptist church split was a result of tension between the Malas and the Madigas. Paul[9] asserts this in his interview with the BASA's Noah Israel. He claims that the caste system within the Indian Baptists characterized the split between Rangiah's group and Lazarus's group. Paul[10] further refers to Chembiah's comments that John Rangiah spoke against sin only to a section of the congregation, the lower class, while his friends, equally guilty of living immoral lives, were overlooked. He goes on to state that the Madigas were treated as the "pariahs," a term for an outcast[11] and were forced to be subservient to the Malas.

While it is true that the lives of these indentured Baptists were shaped by the caste system in India, their arrival in a new country forced them to adapt to a new reality. It was more the traders or passengers than the non-indentured laborers who maintained the caste system. Dhupelia-Mesthrie[12] quotes an indentured laborer as saying, "I have taken my caste and left it with the Port Officer." The passengers on the ships that arrived in South Africa were primarily indentured laborers, free Indians, and passengers. She[13] further asserts that the voyage itself meant breaking the rules of caste. However, the passenger Indians, the vast majority of whom were Gujerati-speaking, had greater links with their country of birth, thus they retained their caste restrictions.[14] Neither Israel's nor Chembiah's comments about the reasons for the split between Rangiah's

5. Power, "Gospel," 1.
6. Ross, "System and Stages."
7. Muthaiah, "Dandora," 1.
8. Joshi, *Untouchables*, 4.
9. Paul, "From Church to Church," 211.
10. Ibid., 212.
11. *Free Dictionary*.
12. Dhupelia-Mesthrie, *From Fields to Freedom*, 13.
13. Ibid., 13.
14. Ibid., 14.

group and Lazarus's group are convincing. Israel provides no details on how this played out, making it difficult to assume that either party used its social status to either demean or feel demeaned.

The records of the BASA and the BMSA do not share the view that Tamils were discriminated against by the Telugus. The writing of the BMSA ex-president Rev. Brian Naidoo[15] and PhD research undertaken by Charles Dayadharum do not share Paul's view that the Tamils were discriminated against by the Telugus.

In analyzing Paul's assertion, it must be noted that in 1978 Paul (a Tamil) himself was elected by the executive council of the Natal Indian Baptist Association to the position of vice-president.[16] His son, Harold T. Paul, is currently the president of this organization.

Dayadharum refutes[17] Paul's hypothesis, arguing that separate churches for Tamils and Baptists did not materialize and that as the Telugu Baptist Church developed, it became inclusive of other sub-cultures, namely the Tamils and the Hindustani. Although Theophilius Rangiah had to deal with the challenge of the caste system, the early pioneers, according to Dayadharum,[18] did well in their efforts to reach out to the different sub-cultures among South African Indians.

Another argument posited by Dayadharum was that among Rangiah's first converts were the Pillay family, who were Tamils. The Pillay children were also among the first pupils in the school Rangiah established. Three of the Pillay sons married John Rangiah's daughters. Thus, Rangiah, it seemed, did not apply the same social rules of endogamy of the caste system.

Though Paul has asserted that Tamils were sidelined by the Telugus, the title of his PhD thesis "From Telugu Baptist Church to Open Church: A Study of the Indian Baptist Missionary Enterprise in South Africa (1903–1989)" suggests an opening of the membership of the Telugu Baptist churches to non-Telugus.

In an article written by John Rangiah, which was a tribute to Lady Hulett, the wife of his landlord, he makes reference to the caste system. He wrote:

15. Naidoo, *Rekindling the Fire*, 27–100.
16. Timothy, *Diamond Jubilee*, 11.
17. Dayadharum, "Role," 128–32.
18. Ibid., 128.

> Regardless of the distinction of caste on one side and color on the other, orphans she guarded and brought them until they became parents of children, by supplying them with food and clothing and medicine while sick; the sick she nursed, the poor she helped, and to the servants she was kind and beneficent.[19]

This reflects Rangiah's awareness of the caste system. His comments suggest that he was affirming Lady Hulett's non-discriminatory attitude towards the different castes. It would therefore seem unlikely that Rangiah encouraged the caste system.

Finally, there is no empirical evidence to support Paul's claim. This—plus Dayadharum's discussion on this issue, the silence in the records of the Baptist Mission of South Africa (including a significant work of Rev. Brian Naidoo, ex-president and ex-general secretary of the BMSA), the fact that Rangiah's three daughters married Tamil-speaking men, and Rangiah's speech on the death of Lady Hullet—weakens Paul's claim that Tamils were discriminated against by Telugus.

---

19. Rangiah, *Report*, 1–5.

6

Women in Ministry within the BASA

JOHN RANGIAH, HIS SON T. M. Rangiah, and David Nathaniel contributed greatly to the BASA. Their respective wives also played important roles. Kanakamma Rangiah served from 1903 to 1931. Sungunamma Rangiah served from 1921 to 1943. Among the women who served is Rajithamma Israel (1956–2006).

There is currently no literature on Indian Baptist women in South Africa. They appear only in BASA brochures. There is little discussion in which their work is assessed and evaluated. I hope to some extent to amend this here.

Although the Rangiahs showed openness to women in ministry, the BASA does not have an official position on this issue. Women were given opportunities to participate in ministry in various capacities. This lack of an official position on women in ministry was shaped largely by apartheid theology, which I will address later. Here, we focus on the contributions of women.

KANAKAMMA RANGIAH, 1903–1931

As mentioned earlier, Kanakamma Rangiah was at first hesitant to accompany her husband, John, to South Africa. But when John arrived in Kearsney to establish the first Indian Baptist Church in South Africa, Kanakamma was part of the leadership team, comprised of John, D. Benjamin, herself and others. She taught the Telugu language to the young girls, and she taught hymns and conducted Bible studies with the women. Kanakamma served as a teacher in the school that Rangiah established in Kearsney, where she provided education to the children of indentured laborers.

An orphanage was started by Mrs. Hullett, the landlady at the tea estate, and Kanakamma was invited to take care of the educational and spiritual needs of these orphans, age twelve to fifteen. She played an important role in teaching the girls to sing, leading worship services, and participating in plays. When the membership of the historic Kearsney Baptist Church increased, a decision was made to construct a larger building. Kanakamma and the women in the congregation assisted in raising financial support for the project. When her husband attended the World Missionary Conference in Edinburgh in 1910, Kanakamma cared for the family, provided leadership to the Kearsney Baptist Church, liaised with leaders of other new established churches, providing counsel and moral and spiritual support to them during her husband's five month absence. A few years later, as the previously discussed church schism unfolded, Kanakamma provided John with the emotional support he needed during that extremely challenging period.

In 1916, when John Rangiah died, Kanakamma had to make some serious decisions about her future ministry with the BASA Church as well as her children's education. She was tempted to return to India but instead stayed to continue the work she and her husband had started. Kanakamma, however, decided to send her ten-year-old son and six-year-old daughter to India so that they could receive a good education.

As noted, Theophilius eventually returned to South Africa. Well-educated, he tended to preach highly academic sermons. Kanakamma guided him and encouraged him to preach simple sermons so that the congregation of mostly indentured laborers could understand him. It is recorded that she once told him after a sermon, "Manoharam, nobody understood you today. Come down to their level."[1]

Kanakamma, after serving for almost twenty-eight years, died on April 13, 1931. Her daughter-in-law, Sungunamma Rangiah, followed in her footsteps.[2]

---

1. Rangiah *NIBA News*, 36.
2. N. M. Israel, telephone communication with the author, 16 September 2007.

SUNGUNAMMA RANGIAH, 1921–1943

Sungunamma Rangiah arrived in South Africa from India with her husband, Theophilius, on March 5, 1921 on board the *SS Umtata*. Sungunamma, an eighteen-year-old girl just out of high school, found it difficult to adjust to the conditions in Natal. Through the support of her mother-in-law, she eventually acclimatized.

Among the significant contributions she and her husband made was the establishment of the BASA Church in Glendale in the Natal North Coast. A woman called "mother Subbamma" was seriously ill and needed healing. It is reported that Sugunamma spent much time in prayer, which resulted in the healing of the woman. This opened more opportunities for healing, which led eventually to the establishment of the new church.

Sungunamma initiated socio-religious work among BASA churches. She taught Telugu and English hymns and choruses. She also held cooking, dressing, and hygiene classes. She was particularly interested in promoting the English language. Young people who passed standard six (grade 8) and who were entering high school were required to preach a sermon in English in the presence of Theophilius and Sungunamma. On Tuesdays, services were held to promote the English language.

Sungunamma opened her house to strangers and to young girls and boys who needed rehabilitation. Her hospitality was especially evident in her ministry to the community at Kearsney, where she and her family lived and served. She played an important role, assisting families in organizing wedding ceremonies, and advising on the choice of jewelry, clothing, and food as well as providing guidance in choosing hymns for the church service. After serving for twenty-three years, Sungunamma died on May 22, 1943. After her death, another woman, Rajithamma Rangiah, John Rangiah's granddaughter, emerged as an important BASA leader.[3]

RAJITHAMMA RANGIAH, 1956–2006

Rajithamma was born at "Gospel Hill" in Kearsney in 1932. She was trained as a school teacher. Wherever she lived, she organized Sunday schools for Indian and Black children. Hindu and Muslim children also attended these Sunday schools. Rajithamma annually prepared these children to write the National Baptist Union Scripture Examinations.

---

3. Israel, telephone communication.

Rajithamma held the position of Assistant Secretary of the BASA for eight years. She also served as president of the BASA Women's Department for twenty-five years. Under her leadership, the Women's Department assisted Bible College students financially, provided financial assistance to churches with building projects, contributed to HIV/AIDS projects, and organized annual women's rallies, special Ascension Day services and spiritual camps for women.

In 2001 Rajithamma initiated a very significant seminar on the "Status of Women in the Church and Community." Another important seminar arranged during her leadership was on HIV/AIDS. She also recognized the need to provide emotional and spiritual support to widows. She organized a widow's fellowship, which became an annual event in the BASA Women's Department.

Rajithamma traveled widely, attending many conferences. In 1975 she attended the Baptist World Alliance Congress in Sweden, where she presented a paper, "Today's Women in South Africa." She also participated in women's conferences in Malawi (2001), Ghana and Brazil (2003); and North Carolina, USA (2003); and attended the Baptist World Alliance Congress in Birmingham, England (2005).

Rajithamma taught young girls the Indian traditional stick dance, which they performed at the 2003 Indian Baptist centenary celebrations at the Durban City Hall. To mark the significance of this centenary celebration, she organized an art competition among the BASA churches where artists were encouraged to depict the historical scenes of the BASA in South Africa. She herself was an art teacher. She also played the role of Kanakamma Rangiah in the radio play, "Behold the Baptist Association of South Africa," produced by Dr. Gabriel Naidoo. The play depicted the life of John Rangiah and was broadcast in three countries—India, Pakistan and South Africa.

Rajithamma continues to this day to serve the church. She continues to sing and promote the singing of Christian hymns in the Telugu language. She also cooperates with other denominations and organizations such as the Tongaat Minister's Fraternal, and she raised funds for the building of a neighboring church in Tongaat. Her work with the BASA spans some fifty years.[4]

---

4. Israel, telephone communication.

In the context of recorded Baptist history that focuses on the contributions of males, the role of women, particularly from the Rangiah family, in the BASA is noteworthy. This is especially true given the challenges of missions in South Africa. These challenges included raising financial support and the promotion of culture and tradition in an African and English context.

MARTHA ISAAC, 1970–1988

It was not only women related to the Rangiahs who played important roles in the Baptist Association of South Africa. Martha Isaac was a locally trained missionary who worked among the women and youth of the BASA. She studied at the Durban Bible College and earned a diploma in theology. Martha rendered spiritual services to women, youth, and children. She was also employed as a missionary of the South African Baptist Missionary Society.[5]

REBECCA RHANDRAM, 1970–2006

Rebecca Rhandram, born Rebecca Peter, is the only daughter of the five children of Mrs. Elsie and Evangelist V. Arumugam Peter. Evangelist Peter, along with Rev. N.E.Tomlinson, founded the South African general mission, now known as the Evangelical Church of South Africa. Rebecca's four brothers followed in their father's footsteps and entered the ministry. Rebecca also took that route. She studied as a full-time student at the Durban Bible College and earned a diploma in theology. In 1968 Rebecca joined the staff of the South African Baptist Missionary Society (now known as the Baptist Missions department of the Baptist Union of Southern Africa) and worked among the Indian churches in Kwa Zulu Natal together with Rev. T. D. Pass, Baptist Union missionary; Miss Judith Morck; Miss Julia Forgus; and Miss Martha Isaac. While with the South African Missionary Society, Rebecca was engaged in the following activities: speaking at ladies' services; daily Vacation Bible Schools in different churches during church holidays; speaking at church youth groups and young women's church groups; teaching in church and wayside Sunday schools; and visiting church members and counseling those who wanted to put their faith in Christ. Rebecca resigned from the South African

---

5. D. Ragwan, letter to author, 9 September 2008.

Baptist Missionary Society in December of 1971 when she married The Rev. T. Rhandram, who is currently a Baptist minister.[6]

ESTHER BENJAMIN, 1970–2006

Esther, unlike Martha and Rebecca, did not receive any formal training in mission work but worked with the BASA as a missionary. She contributed to the women's ministry of the BASA, serving as vice president of the women's organization. Her extensive travels included many short-term missions to Malawi, Swaziland, and Mozambique.[7]

VALERIE DAYANANDHUM, 1989–2006

Valerie was the great-granddaughter of David Rajanna, who came to South Africa as an indentured laborer from India. He was the pastor of the Tinley Manor Baptist Church. Valerie, a graduate of Durban Bible College, served as president of the Baptist Women's

Department of the BASA. Her activities included working with women, speaking at youth and women's retreats, preaching, and leading worship. She also served as a BASA missionary. Valerie participated in short-term missions to Swaziland, Malawi, and Mozambique.[8]

MARGE NATHANIEL, 1998–2003

Marge Nathaniel is the daughter-in-law of the late Rev. D. N. Nathaniel. She is from a Catholic background, but married the youngest son of Rev. and Mrs. Nathaniel. Marge trained as a school teacher and in 1998 was elected as the first female general secretary of the BASA, playing an important role in the administrative affairs of the organization. She also addressed the organization at significant events. Marge possessed the gift of communication as she ably articulated the vision of the organization. Marge was responsible for initiating important workshops and conferences, most notably on Leadership.[9]

---

6. T. Rhandram, letter to author, 9 September 2008.
7. Ragwan, letter to author.
8. Ibid.
9. Swamy, *Brochure*, 10–11.

EVELYN MAISTRY, 1990–2006

Although BASA did not formally recognize women ministers, a local church of BASA called Living Stones Baptist Church inducted the first woman minister. Then-BASA president Anthony Poliah inducted Evelyn Maistry into ministry. Mrs. Maistry served in various capacities in BASA, most notably as vice president of the Baptist Women's Department and director of the Christian Education department. In 2003, she also traveled to the USA to participate in ministry and workshops that were planned by BASA.[10]

THE BASA AND WOMEN IN MINISTRY

Although BASA has allowed women to engage in ministry, it has not formally put into place a policy with regard to women in ministry. It still largely reflects a hierarchical model in its ministries, which no doubt was influenced by apartheid theology.

The contributions of women to the Indian Baptist work in South Africa are noteworthy given the view held by many of the churches during this period. However, this view still fell short of the biblical view of women. Although BASA allowed women to engage in ministry, it reflected a view that women were not equal to men. This view was a result of the Scriptural hermeneutic of church leaders both in BASA and in the other South African Baptist organizations. In the South African context, the question of how to interpret the creation of human persons became an issue that influenced how Baptists viewed women in ministry. Faced with this question of interpretation, White Christians, and more specifically the Afrikaner Christians, claimed that they were the ones who could interpret the Biblical text. They also believed that they were responsible for passing their interpretation of Scripture on to people of color.

People of color had no participation in the formulation and construction of theology and, furthermore, were not allowed to criticize the theology that was passed on to them. South Africans of all races were influenced by apartheid theology, which, in addition to its restrictive framework, applied racial and gender stereotypes to human persons. According to apartheid theology, white persons are superior to Blacks, Indians, and so-called Coloreds, and men are considered superior to women. This theology has been oppressive and dehumanizing.

10. Ragwan, letter to author.

The question of alternative Scriptural understandings of the role and status of women—in the home and in the church—is a topic for another book. In fact, many books and essays from Christian thinkers across the theological spectrum have addressed this topic. New Testament scholar Manfred Brauch, for example, makes a compelling case for the full equality of women in the church and in the home. It is my hope that teachers and laypersons—not only in South Africa but all over the world—will become familiar with the views of Brauch and many others, views with strong scriptural support, so that the change that is needed in this area can occur.

7

The BASA and Unity Talks

THE HISTORIC EMERGENCE OF an indigenous Indian Baptist mission in South Africa occurred in an era of European expansion, colonialism, and apartheid. During this long period, South Africa's major population groups—Blacks, Coloreds, Indians, and Whites—were racially divided. Throughout this period there was no significant movement among Baptists towards racial reconciliation. There were, however, conversations between the predominantly White Baptist Union of South Africa and the Black Baptist Convention of South Africa as well as between the two ethnic Indian Baptist groups: the Baptist Association of South Africa and the Baptist Mission of South Africa. However, these conversations were not inclusive. The conversations between the White and Black Baptists had to be terminated at the request of the members of the Indian and Afrikaans as they excluded the Indian and Afrikaans Baptists.

The political climate in South Africa in the 1990s provided the conditions for all races to engage one another and work towards reconciliation. In 1994 a new era dawned in South Africa. The release of Nelson Mandela from prison further created an opportunity for all South Africans to embrace reconciliation. In 1999 the leaders of the five Baptist organizations recognized this defining moment and began a process of dialogue with one another.

It was a new beginning for South African Baptists, as Baptists from the five racially divided groups—the Baptist Convention of South Africa, the Baptist Union of South Africa, the Baptist Association of South Africa, the Baptist Mission of South Africa, and the Afrikanse Baptiste Kerk (an

Afrikaans-speaking organization) began a process of engagement on reconciliation and unity.[1] Before discussing the participation and contribution of BASA in this process, we must first locate BASA within the larger social and political framework and show how it was influenced by that framework.

THE DUTCH PERIOD

The history of the church in South Africa is best understood in terms of three phases: the Dutch Period (1652–1795), the British Period (1795/1814/1948) and the Afrikaner Period (1924/1948–47).

Jan van Riebeeck was dispatched by the Dutch East India Company (DEIC) to build a fort and establish a garden at the Cape. In 1652 he established a refreshment station,[2] which served as a halfway station for ships between Holland and the East. The purpose of this venture was to increase the profit of the DEIC's trade and small-scale farming. According to Regehr,[3] van Riebeeck had no interest in conquest and subjugation.

During the Dutch occupation of the Cape, slave labor was introduced. In 1658 West Africans were first used as slaves, and later the DEIC added to its African slave numbers slaves from territories such as India (particularly from Bengal and the Coromandel and Malabar Coasts) and from the Indonesian islands. Dhupelia-Mesthrie[4] writes about a young boy in the seventeenth century named Ari, who was playing on a beach on the west coast of Bengal when he was captured and taken as a slave to the Cape where he became a possession of the Dutch. Many other Indians like Ari were brought as slaves to the Cape, and married other slaves from the East, from Africa, or from among the indigenous Khoisan inhabitants. The early Dutch settlers depended upon the Khoisan inhabitants for their cattle. The Khoisan people were nomadic; they followed their herds of cattle and sheep to grazing areas. They later became known as the Hottentots.[5]

As these communities lived side by side, the Dutch settlers initiated the first sign of apartheid by erecting a hedge separating the Khoisan from the Dutch settlement. Further conflict between the two communi-

---

1. I examined this unity process in my 2004 Master of Arts thesis, "An Inquiry into the Unity Process among Baptists in South Africa."
2. Dvorin, *Separation*, 10.
3. Regehr, *Perceptions*, 105.
4. Dhupelia-Mesthrie, *From Fields to Freedom*, 10.
5. Regehr, *Perceptions*, 105.

ties arose over grazing rights and land. This eventually led to two wars, forcing the Khoisan to accept the Dutch occupation. The Dutch hired the Khoisan as farm laborers and domestic servants. As a result of miscegenation between the San, Khoisan, slaves, and whites, the colored population (people of mixed blood) emerged.[6] Dhupelia-Mesthrie's[7] contention that Indian slaves who were brought to the Cape by the Dutch resulted in the miscegenation between the Indians and the San and Khoisans (which brought about the Colored people) is worthy of further examination.

Despite the mixing of races during this period, the whites, according to Loubser,[8] viewed themselves as distinct. Loubser further stated that in 1788, a number of Stellenbosch people protested against a corporal who was "of dark and of heathen descent." At the end of the eighteenth century, race prejudice was firmly established everywhere. Shortly after this the Afrikaans language became a symbol of white identity.[9]

The Bible played a part in the lives of the settlers as it guided and informed life in the colony. During the Dutch period, the public expression of Christianity was largely monopolized by the Dutch Reformed Church, closely overseen by the ruling Dutch East India Company. Elphick and Davenport[10] argue that most social historians do not fully recognize that Reformed piety and doctrine were influential in the shaping of White society as well as of White-Black relations.

THE BRITISH ERA

Generally, many have been critical of the Afrikaner because the Afrikaner is synonymous with apartheid. One must assign some blame to the British for the divisions in South Africa. I recall as a student attending a lecture in 1986 by evangelical scholar John Stott to the student body of the Baptist Theological College of Southern Africa in Parktown, Johannesburg. The subject was apartheid and the Christian's response to it. Stott shared the lecture with a few local English speakers. During the question-and-answer sessions, the Afrikaners were blamed for apartheid. A fellow Black student confronted the speakers about the role the English had played

---

6. Stack and Morton, *Torment to Triumph*, 11.
7. Dhupelia-Mesthrie, *From Fields to Freedom*, 10.
8. Loubser, *Bible*, 5.
9. Davenport, *South Africa*, 5.
10. Ibid., 2.

in the divisions in South Africa, which led to confessions and apologies. On the other hand it should be stated that some British promoted racial harmony. Some took issue with the Boers' treatment of Blacks.

According to Loubser,[11] within a decade the Cape suffered a change of government three times (1795/1803/1806), and each time the church had to adapt itself to new situations. In 1806, when the British took control of South Africa, little changed for Blacks. The British passed restrictive laws that suppressed most Blacks, took away most of their land, and made them dependent on Europeans in order to make them subservient to White Rule.[12] Regehr[13] on the other hand, argued that during this period Blacks experienced more freedom, as they could now enter the colony freely under a pass system to sell labor and trade. He cites Dr. John Philip's work among the Blacks. Dr. Philip championed the cause of the Blacks and was not well received by the Boers because of his influence on the government regarding the issue of Ordinance 50, which supported Blacks enjoying the same legal rights that White colonists enjoyed.[14] Although he advanced the course of the Khoisan, Philip felt that Blacks should live separate from Whites until such time as they could compete with Whites in White culture on equal footing. Regehr[15] also stated that John Philip wanted African chiefs to safeguard their land from the incursion of White farmers.

There were further attempts by the English to advance their imperialistic supremacy. They attempted, unsuccessfully, to anglicize the Dutch. However, Regehr stated[16] that the Afrikaans language became dominant among the "colored" people.

During this period, apartheid was introduced by the National Party when it came into power in 1948.[17] Apartheid became legally sanctioned.

APARTHEID'S INFLUENCE ON THE BAPTIST CHURCH

The single most disuniting force among Baptists in South Africa has been apartheid. It manifested itself in many ways in the church, such as inferior

---

11. Loubser, *Bible*, 5.
12. Ngcokovane, *Apartheid*, 2.
13. Regehr, *Perceptions*, 121.
14. Ibid., 121.
15. Ibid.
16. Ibid., 116.
17. Stack and Morton, *Torment to Triumph*, 16.

theological education for Blacks, insensitivity of white Baptists towards black Baptists, and structures of the white Baptist Union of South Africa that were considered to be racist.

The papers presented at the BCSA's Awareness Workshop, held in Barkly West in 1990, reflect the claim of the Baptist Convention of South Africa that the Baptist Union of South Africa still practiced racism and apartheid within its structures and ministries. One would have thought that the church would be free from the influence of this ideology as the democratic forces in the country were challenging the apartheid ideology. Unfortunately, apartheid brought about much conflict between black and white Baptists. It also allowed other Baptists, such as the Afrikaanse Baptiste Kerk, the Baptist Mission of South Africa, and BASA to remain separate.

Before providing more details on the disunity among the five Baptist groups, I will define apartheid and racism and describe apartheid ideology. Apartheid, literally translated, means "apart-ness" or "separation." Pronounced "apar-hate", the term was first used in a leading Afrikaans newspaper in 1943.[18] Dr. Malan, the first Nationalist prime minister, used it frequently to describe South Africa's goals of government. Central to this system was the notion that the different races and cultures of South Africa could never be an integrated whole sharing a common citizenship. The whites (English and Afrikaans-speaking) perpetuated apartheid while Blacks, Indians, and Coloreds were on the "receiving end" of this ideology.

Stack and Morton[19] describe apartheid and its effects on the black population of South Africa, and his description provides a sense of the conditions of apartheid under which both black and white Christians, including Baptists, had to live out their faith. Black people were forcibly removed from their land and given arid tribal "homelands." They were stripped of their right to vote even as the all-white government controlled their destinies. They were reduced to offering their labor at poverty wages to gain the right to re-enter the "white" land (white people owned eighty-seven percent of the land) where they worked, separated from their families eleven months out of the year as migrant laborers.[20]

The fruits of the apartheid state accrued mainly to the Whites, who swallowed up almost seventy percent of the total national income.

18. Ibid., 17.
19. Ibid.
20. Ibid., 17–18.

Apartheid was all about a life of privilege, power, and plenty for Whites, based on the exploitation of cheap "non-White" labor. Martin M. Marger, in his book *Race and Ethnic Relations,* states that the cruel irony of apartheid was that it was financed primarily by its victims. All non-Whites—Africans, Coloreds and Indians—were discriminated against, yet they had to underwrite the oppressive system by accepting artificially low wages and seriously deprived working and living arrangements.[21]

In reality, the entire population were daily victims in one sense or another. Blacks suffered daily disasters, from homicide to humiliation. I myself was thrown out of a first-class coach while travelling from Johannesburg to Germiston because of the color of my skin, as the first-class coach was reserved for Whites only.[22] From expropriation to grinding poverty, from brutal torture and imprisonment to relentless persecution, family life was shattered, careers wrecked, and education withheld. Life consisted of round-the-clock survival. According to Stack and Morton,[23] even supporters of apartheid paid a price, living in constant fear that they had created a monster and were losing basic human sensitivity. Perhaps the best way to describe apartheid is to read the words of two Prime ministers, Mr. Strijdom and Mr. Verwoerd:

> Our policy is that the Europeans must stand their ground and must remain baas (boss) in South Africa. If we reject the Herrenvolk idea and the idea that the White man cannot remain baas, if the franchise is to be extended to the non-Europeans, and if the non-Europeans are developed on the same basis as the Europeans, how can the European remain baas? Our view is that in every sphere we must retain the right to rule the country and keep it a White man's country.[24]

T. R. H. Davenport, in his book *South Africa: Modern History,* confirms this by stating[25] that the mystique of apartheid, as elaborated by its proponents after 1948, came to mean separation in all possible fields—political, territorial, residential, cultural, and economic. Analysis of such a state-

---

21. Marger, *Race and Relations,* 440.
22. Ragwan, *Service,* 19.
23. Stack and Morton, *Torment to Triumph,* 18.
24. Ibid.
25. Davenport, *South* Africa, 331.

ment makes it clear that the principles of apartheid clearly advocated the separation of races.

Stack and Morton recorded[26] Mr. Verwoerd's speech in the House of Assembly on January 25, 1963 in which he stated, "Reduced to its simplest form the problem is nothing else than this: We want to keep South Africa White. Keeping it White can only mean one thing, namely White domination, not leadership, not guidance, but control, supremacy." Here, too, the strong insistence was that South Africa be a country with separate races with Whites enjoying supremacy over Blacks, Coloreds, and Indians. The church could not help but be adversely affected by this reality.

It could be said that the idea of racial separation started in the late 1800s, though many would be tempted to suggest that it started in 1948 when the National Party came to power with its racist policies. De Gruchy[27] states that the settler church (and in particular the Dutch Reformed Church's missionary program through its custom and culture) provided an ecclesiological blueprint for the nationalistic policy of separate development. The British, too, joined in by perpetuating this ideology as will be seen later. It is within such a milieu that Baptists began their work.

It should also be stated that Baptists were among the settlers who came to South Africa. Hudson-Reed[28] confirms this by stating, "Among the intrepid British Settlers of 1820 was a small group of Baptist laymen." Baptists, too, were influenced by the colonial missionary model and were divided along racial and ethnic lines. It may seem unfair to single out two of the organizations, the BUSA and the ABK, that historically enjoyed full citizenship and were protected by the law of the land; the reality is that they benefited from such a system.

History records that the five Baptist organizations began in different periods. BUSA was formed in 1877,[29] ABK in 1944,[30] BCSA in 1927,[31] BASA in 1914[32] and BMSA in 1903.[33]

---

26. Stack and Morton, *Torment to Triumph*, 17.
27. De Gruchy, *Struggle*, 9.
28. Hudson-Reed, *By Taking Heed*, 15.
29. Ibid., 361.
30. Ibid., 218.
31. Hoffmeister and Gurney, *Workshop*, 33.
32. Rangiah, *NIBA News*, 10.
33. Jacob and Cornelius, *Brochure*, 3.

78 VISION IN PROGRESS

It should be noted that apartheid occurred in a country populated by a majority of Blacks.[34] The population groups of South Africa were separated from each other politically, socially, culturally, and territorially along racial lines. Racism played a major role in this process. Apartheid meant the separation of Blacks in every field.

RACISM

Having looked at an ideological system that caused so much division, we now examine another phenomenon, racism, which also adversely affected the population of South Africa. The term "race" is defined by A. S. Park in his book *Racial Conflict and Healing* as "group of human beings possessing in common certain physical characteristics which are determined by heredity." He further states that racism is the "dogma that one ethnic group is condemned by nature to congenital inferiority and another group to congenital superiority."[35] Denton Lotz, the former General Secretary of the Baptist World Alliance,[36] defined racism as being rooted in the belief that a group or groups of people are by heredity and nature intrinsically superior to the rest of humankind. Racism demands, supports, and legitimizes the use of power in order to define, devalue, dominate and discriminate against those considered inferior.

Lotz[37] answers an important question of why racism is a worldwide problem. He states that racism has existed from the beginning of human history in very different forms. He contends[38] that this is shown in "rudimentary drawings on the walls of prehistoric caves and paintings in Egyptian tombs." Lauren, in his book *Power and Prejudice*, likewise maintains that discrimination is ancient in its origins. He maintains that from the earliest periods of human existence, groups developed prejudices towards others and then discriminated against those they regarded as different or inferior.[39]

---

34. Stack and Morton, *Torment to Triumph*, 10.
35. Park, *Conflict and Healing*, 24.
36. Lotz, *Baptists*, 22.
37. Ibid., 9.
38. Ibid., 10.
39. Lauren, *Power and Prejudice*, 5.

According to Lotz,[40] the real problem of the twentieth century would be the problem of the color line—the relation of the darker to the lighter races. He highlights[41] information from the Human Rights Watch World Report of 1993 where racial and ethnic conflicts around the world have taken place. They include Somalia (the violent Destruction caused by fighting among the clans and subclans); Sri Lanka (the Sinhalese against the Tamil minority, resulting in 1.5 million displaced persons); Sudan (the Arab North against the Black animist/Christian South); Turkey (the Turkish majority against the minority Kurds); Iraq (Iraqis against the Kurds); Palestine (the Arab-Israeli conflict); Kenya (tribal tensions); Nigeria (ethnic conflicts); Germany (conflict with foreign workers); Myanmar (conflict with the Muslim minority and tribal aspirations); Mauritania (Arab-Berber government used fraud and violence to disenfranchise a large number of Blacks).

The European people, after setting foot on African soil, were involved in a racial conflict and a struggle for survival. Loubser wrote[42] that because of their European background they were totally unprepared for life in a new country. To add to their frustrations, the Afrikaners did not favor racial integration of the churches; this divided the Dutch Reformed Church and the English-speaking churches.

De Gruchy[43] elaborates further on the struggles of the Afrikaner against British imperialism. This frustration and unhappiness of the Afrikaner with British imperialism led them to trek northwards with a hope of building their own permanent nation.[44] This outrage and frustration is reflected in the words of a Voortreker woman named Anna Steenkamp:

It is not so much their freeing which drove us to such lengths, as their being placed on equal footing with Christians, contrary to the laws of God, and the natural distinction of race and color so that it was intolerable for any decent Christian to bow down beneath such a yoke, wherefore we rather withdrew in order to preserve our doctrines of purity.[45]

---

40. Lotz, *Baptists*, 9.
41. Ibid., 9–11.
42. Loubser, *Bible*, 3.
43. De Gruchy, *Struggle*, 18.
44. Regehr, *Perceptions*, 103.
45. De Gruchy, *Struggle*, 19.

The real reason for the Afrikaners trekking away from British control may be a theological one, though this can be disputed. According to Hexman, most agree that the ideological roots of Afrikaner Nationalism are to be found in the Calvinist religion of the early White settlers who arrived at the Cape of Good Hope in the mid-seventeenth century.[46]

Hexham further claims that another factor that played a continuing role in holding the Afrikaner people together and shaping their philosophy is the Calvinism preached and practiced by the three largest Afrikaner Reformed churches, of which ninety percent of Afrikaners were adherents. The Old Testament was like a mirror of their own lives. In it they found the deserts and fountains, the droughts and plagues, the captivity and the exodus. Above all they found a chosen people guided by a stern but loving deity through the midst of the heathen to a promised land.

Hexham says that the Old Testament and the doctrines of Calvin molded the Boer into the Afrikaner of today. This exclusive and sectarian view of themselves did very little to improve race relations, which for decades had become an impediment to a free and just South Africa. This divisive system of apartheid had an adverse effect on the Baptist church in South Africa as well, as by this time all five Baptist organizations were in existence.

Hoffmeister and Gurney cite Louise Kretzschmar's paper, "A Theology of Dominance: an Alternative History of the Baptist Union of South Africa," which she presented at the 1990 BWAW. In it, she recalls[47] a settler type ideology in a pamphlet of the BUSA. In the pamphlet it is said that the Baptist settlers "ventured the stormy seas of the Cape where the scattered settlers were too few to keep the kaffirs to their agreed upon eastern side of the Great Fish River. They treated their pledges as scraps of paper, and when it pleased them they crossed the river to plunder cattle."

The Baptist settlers seemed to regard their possession of the land as being justified on the spurious grounds that the Xhosas were treaty breakers, cattle thieves and invaders. The repetition of such views in the recent years, says Kretzschmar,[48] is completely unjustifiable. C. M. Wilson, in his book *Co-operation and Conflict: The Eastern Frontier*, agrees with Kretzschmar by referring to the findings of a historical analysis. He

---

46. Hexham, *Irony*, 1.
47. Hoffmeister and Gurney, *Workshop*, 27.
48. Ibid., 27.

states[49] that the extent of these treaties was greatly misunderstood by both the settlers and colonial authorities, that the Xhosa were not the only cattle thieves, and that the series of border conflicts were, at least in part, desperate attempts by the Xhosa to defend what remained of their land.

In the recording of the histories of the five Baptist organizations by their respective historians, all but the Baptist Convention of South Africa write about the social, political, and economic injustices that apartheid created. Instead, BCSA highlights its achievements, victories, and strides it has made as Baptists in South Africa. Hudson-Reed's recording of the BUSA is one such example. In his view[50] the Baptist history, particularly BUSA history, is an outstanding one. While from a BUSA perspective it has been an outstanding one, the reality is that the history of Baptists in South Africa has been one of division that for many years existed along racial lines.

THE CHURCH'S RESPONSE TO APARTHEID

How did the Christian church respond to the problem of apartheid, which contributed to the disunity of the church as well as to the disunity among the country's peoples? Although there were racial divisions in South Africa prior to 1948 not much was being done by the church to address this problem. De Gruchy[51] stated that generally the church in South Africa prior to 1948 was preoccupied with the desire for peace. The Christian Council, which was formed in 1936 to foster cooperation among the churches, had called a conference at the University of Fort Hare in 1940 to discuss the task of the churches in "Christian Reconstruction" after the war.[52] It seemed that after the war with Hitler the world would be at peace. Seven years later the Christian Council convened another conference, this time at Rosettenville in Johannesburg. The theme was "The Church in a Multi-Racial Society." De Gruchy recorded that the optimism of Fort Hare had gone. The mood was one of apprehension. Apartheid had arrived.[53]

---

49. Wilson, *History*, 233.
50. Hudson-Reed, *By Taking Heed*, 7.
51. De Gruchy, *Struggle*, 39.
52. Ibid.
53. Ibid., 53.

How did Baptists in South Africa respond? The conference convened by the Christian Council in 1949 invited leaders from various denominations, including Baptists, to deal with the church's response to apartheid. BASA was not invited; BUSA represented the Baptist denomination. Given its position on various political issues as well as the all-white government, BUSA would not have been a fully representative voice, and therefore most likely would not offer a strong opposition to apartheid. Furthermore, BUSA, according to De Gruchy,[54] generally was more cautious on political matters. From 1949 to 1990, the BUSA continued to be cautious.

In 1990 the mainly Black Baptist Convention of South Africa convened a workshop to deal with the issue of apartheid and to come up with a way forward. Most of the Black Baptists' response was expressed at a workshop held in 1990 in Barkly West, called the Barkly West Awareness Workshop (BWAW). This workshop brought together leaders who applied their minds to working out an "empowered future." In doing so they attempted to come to terms with, in the words of the editors Rev. Desmond Hoffmeister and Brian Gurney,[55] the "official history of Baptist witness in South Africa." It was also stated that apartheid had wound itself into the structures of the Baptist witness in Southern Africa.[56] This workshop dealt mainly with the BCSA's response to the history of the BUSA, which in the opinion of Hoffmeister and Gurney was racist.

At this BWAW conference, the BCSA listed the effects of apartheid on the Baptist Convention. It lists first the training of their pastors. BCSA pastors were first trained at Millard Bible School in Orlando, Soweto. The school was later relocated to Ciskei. This relocation was motivated by apartheid as the government wanted to remove Blacks from the urban areas.[57] Stack and Morton,[58] in their book *Torment to Triumph,* explain the Influx Control Act, which stipulates that no African be permitted to remain in an urban area for longer than seventy-two hours without a permit, unless he or she was born there and has been continuously resident. Exceptions were made for persons who worked in one area continuously for ten years for one employer or for fifteen years for more than one employer.

54. Ibid., 61.
55. Hoffmeister and Gurney, *Workshop,* 5.
56. Ibid.
57. Ibid., 54.
58. Stack and Morton, *Torment to Triumph,* 26.

Black pastors of the BCSA received inferior theological education. Hoffmeister[59] bemoaned the criteria applied by the then-White Baptist Union, which stated, "It is desirable that a candidate should have passed at least the equivalent education of junior (standard eight)." With regards to the training of the BCSA pastors, he says, "Theological training of Convention pastors was subjected to the standards imposed by the Baptist Union. Our potential was limited. The curriculum was foreign in all respects. It became an insult to our dignity and humanness."[60]

Kretzschmar[61] calls the education at these institutions both Euro-centered and privatized. By this she meant that the questions, subject matter, books, and lecturers were predominantly based on European and North American theology. Further criticism of the theological education received by the BCSA pastors, according to Kretzschmar, was that students were not exposed to the significance of the rise of African and Black theologies. She adds that social ethics, especially issues directly related to the South African context, received little or no emphasis. It is quite obvious that the pastors trained at a Black theological school were not being adequately prepared to minister within a context of political oppression and economic deprivation. Nor were they given the tools to evaluate the BUSA's own perception of the Christian gospel.[62]

When reading De Gruchy's recording[63] of the Baptist Union's statement to the apartheid government after the government wanted to deprive Africans of their limited Parliamentary representation, one is tempted to come to the defense of the BUSA. Hoffmeister, however,[64] argued that no practical steps were taken by BUSA to challenge the state. Nevertheless, BUSA, together with the Presbyterian Church of South Africa, the Methodists and the Congregational Assembly, stated its opposition to the government's proposed legislation aimed at depriving Africans of their limited Parliamentary representation. According to De Gruchy[65] the Assembly of the Baptist Union condemned this proposed

---

59. Hoffmeister and Gurney, *Workshop*, 54.
60. Ibid.
61. Ibid., 30.
62. Ibid.
63. De Gruchy, *Struggle*, 54.
64. Hoffmeister and Gurney, *Workshop*, 28.
65. De Gruchy, *Struggle*, 54.

legislation by stating that "any tampering with the accepted constitutional understanding that the franchise rights of non-Europeans will continue to be entrenched as provided in the South Africa Act. Furthermore it was gravely concerned at the rising tide of bitterness and resentment, non-cooperation and hatred, which is evident among those people concerned, by any suggestion of the limitation of their existing rights and legitimate aspirations, and the Assembly resolutely dissociates itself from any policy which would restrict or reduce the present rights of representation in Parliament or Senate of any section of the community."[66]

The above statement to the government was not the only one wherein BUSA expressed concern about apartheid laws. Over the years there have been individuals within the BUSA who have supported statements made at its Annual Assembly, statements critical of the government. Or they addressed letters to the State resident and other officials. As mentioned earlier, one is tempted to come to BUSA's defense as one reads its criticism of apartheid laws. However, Kretzschmar[67] in a paper presented at the BCSA's Awareness Workshop titled "A Theology of Dominance: An Alternative History of the South African Baptist Union," helps us understand the level of commitment the BUSA truly had in opposing apartheid. Kretzschmar[68] states, "But to agree to a statement of protest at Assembly is one thing; to devise practical steps to implement such protest is quite another."

This indicated a lack of commitment by the BUSA to address and help remove the injustices of apartheid. It could be said in the words of Villa-Vicencio's[69] reference to the protests of most English-speaking churches: "Their protest was neither harsh nor rigorous." Kretzchmar[70] further cited another discriminatory practice employed by the BUSA. A close examination of the BUSA's mission policies indicated discrimination and White domination. This was, according to her, revealed in its missions policies. Rather than pursuing a policy of partnership in mission or practicing a form of mission that included concern for the material needs of communities, mission was conceived of as evangelism by Whites to Blacks. The

---

66. Ibid., 54–55.
67. Hoffmeister and Gurney, *Workshop*, 24–31.
68. Ibid., 28.
69. Villa-Vicencio, *Trapped*, 1.
70. Hoffmeister and Gurney, *Workshop*, 29.

South African Baptist Missionary Society (SABMS), which was a division of the BUSA, undertook the mission work of the BUSA, and the Black churches that were started by BUSA fell under the control of the SABMS. Increasingly the pattern of separate churches for different races became entrenched. Kretzchmar continued in her criticism of the BUSA by stating that these churches under the SABMS had very little representation on the BUSA executive committee and were subject to the policy decisions of these bodies and of the White missionary superintendents.[71]

The listing of the Baptist ministers in the BUSA handbook along racial lines illustrates apartheid practiced by the BUSA. Kretzchmar notes that the BUSA stated in its 1976 Assembly: "Assembly reaffirmed that the Baptist Union of South Africa is open to all churches which desire to join it and which qualify in terms of the constitution, regardless of race or color." It affirmed that such churches would be welcomed into the Union and charged the executive committee to make this known to all churches within the Baptist Union Associations. Yet the BUSA had the names of Black ministers listed separately.

Racial discrimination was reflected also in the BUSA 1989 Assembly, which was held in Kimberley. Racially separate accommodation was provided for all delegates. The venue of this Kimberley Assembly, which was held in a military barracks, was hurtful to the Black members of the BUSA who attended. The military in South Africa was an instrument of the apartheid state that crushed anti-apartheid activists. The Baptist Union was accused of being insensitive to Blacks, as the venue was a symbol of White oppression and violence. This resulted in the walkout of Blacks in protest against the BUSA.

ETHNICITY

Cornell and Hartman, in their book *Ethnicity and Race,* observe that the word "ethnic" has a long history and that it is a derivative of the Greek word *ethnos,* meaning "nation." The term "ethnic" was previously thought of as race or nation. In English the word "ethnic" referred to someone who was neither Christian nor Jewish, in other words, a pagan or heathen.[72] These terms, according to Marger,[73] are clearly different in meaning.

71. Ibid., 28–29.
72. Cornell and Hartman, *Ethnicity and Race,* 16.
73. Marger, *Race and Relations,* 10.

Marger[74] draws our attention to the fact that ethnic groups are groups within a larger society that display a unique set of cultural traits. Marger draws on the comments of Melvin Tumin, a sociologist who provides a definition of an ethnic group as a "social group, which, within a larger cultural and social system, claims or is accorded special status in terms of a complex of traits (ethnic traits), which it exhibits or is believed to exhibit." It can be said that ethnic groups are subcultures that maintain certain behavioral characteristics that in some degree set them apart from society's mainstream culture.

Three of the five Baptist organizations—BASA, BMSA, and ABK—fall into the category of ethnic group. The ABK, which represented Afrikaans-speaking people, held dearly to their own language and culture. According to Reed,[75] the ABK is a language-union of the BUSA, meaning that its members spoke Afrikaans.

Marger's second assertion[76] is that in addition to a common sharing of cultural traits, ethnic groups display a sense of community among members. He says that there is a consciousness of kind or awareness of close association. Gordon Milton, in his book *Assimilation in American Life*, suggests that the ethnic group serves, above all, as a social-psychological referent in creating a "sense of peoplehood." He further states that this sense of community, or oneness, derives from an understanding of a shared ancestry or heritage and that ethnic groups view themselves as having common roots.[77]

Manhoran Rangiah, the grandson of John Rangiah, in his editorial comments in the *Natal Indian Baptist Golden Jubilee Brochure*, supports Marger's suggestion that in ethnic groups there is a sense of community, derived from an understanding of a shared ancestry or heritage. M. Rangiah stated:

> NIBA is our sacred heritage handed to us by those who have gone before us. By the grace of God, we have, with all our limitations and inadequacies, guarded the interests of the Association jealously, upheld its traditions sacredly, its principles resolutely and kept aflame the spirit our forebears put into the Association. May

---

74. Ibid., 11.
75. Hudson-Reed, *By Taking Heed*, 218.
76. Marger, *Race and Relations*, 11.
77. Milton, *Assimilation*, 84.

we be privileged to hand over this cherished heritage to our children when we depart from them."[78]

In analyzing Rangiah's critique of Marger's definition,[79] it is very clear that he was reflecting ethnic characteristics. BASA has remained largely an ethnic Baptist organization since 1914. While BASA is a member of the South African Baptist Alliance, any suggestion to form a united Baptist organization will not be easily accepted by this organization.[80] As far as the BMSA is concerned, it has indicated that it is ready and willing to form one united Baptist body. Although BMSA is also largely an ethnic organization, it remains to be seen what influence ethnicity will play when Baptists finally agree to form that one united Baptist organization in South Africa. It would be naïve to think that ethnicity has not influenced the unification process in South Africa. As was stated, the three ethnic Baptist organizations held strongly to their traditions, heritage and, in one case, language. The true test will come when structural unity becomes a reality among Baptists in South Africa.

SABA has allowed for the five Baptist organizations to engage one another in the area of unity and cooperation. However, there is a past that was painful and challenging. The relationship of the ABK, BASA, BSCA and BMSA with the BUSA had its challenges and at times caused pain. Each of these four organizations' respective relationships with BUSA will now be examined.

THE ABK AND THE BUSA

The Afrikanse Baptiste Kerk (ABK) was an ethnic and language union of the BUSA. Although strong representations were made by the ABK to the BUSA to discuss having its own legal entity, these attempts were unsuccessful. It was accepted that the ABK, because of language and cultural differences, should make provision for the expansion of its own membership.[81]

Hudson-Reed, in his book *By Taking Heed*, records the relationship between the BUSA and the ABK. He states that the stunted growth of the Baptist community among the Afrikaans-speaking people is attributable in large measure to the sometimes negative and unsympathetic attitude

---

78. Rangiah *NIBA News*, 2.
79. Marger, *Race and Relations*, 11.
80. SABA Minutes 1999, 6.
81. Hudson-Reed, *By Taking Heed*, 218.

of the BUSA. Despite this, a good relationship between the two organizations followed. Tensions arose when the BUSA formulated a strongly worded resolution to the National Party that came into power in 1948, a resolution focusing on race relations. Reed records the disappointment of the ABK regarding these resolutions. The ABK regarded these actions as unwarranted and felt that the BUSA was meddling in politics. Furthermore, these resolutions, according to Hudson-Reed, proved to be a real obstacle to reaching Afrikaners with the Gospel.[82]

Relationships with the BUSA deteriorated, and in 1960 a BUSA delegation visited the ABK to discuss its relationship with the Union. The purpose of this meeting was also to find ways of overcoming misunderstandings and to establish better relationships. The Committee of the BUSA recommended to the ABK that it consider the formation of a separate Baptist Union. The motivation for such a recommendation is recorded by Hudson-Reed as follows:

1. the ABK's attitude with regard to race relations;
2. the frustration experienced in some congregations on account of the limited representation on the Baptist Union's Executive Committee;
3. the importance of the development of Baptists among Afrikaans-speaking people;
4. the foundation of the Seminarium as an official training center of the ABK;
5. the fact that the ABK already functions as an independent Union.

The BUSA executive committee did not accept this resolution. A recommendation was made to the BUSA to strengthen the bonds of unity. In assessing this relationship, the BUSA still had some control over certain matters, including that ministers of the ABK would be interviewed by the BUSA, all applications for marriage licenses would be made by the General Secretary of BUSA, and the minutes of the ABK would be sent to BUSA. It must be stressed here that, although the ABK remained an integral part of the BUSA, it functioned as a separate association. Furthermore the BUSA did not make any provision for representation of ethnic and language groups within the BUSA. The BUSA promised the ethnic groups that they would be consulted from time to time. Hudson-

---

82. Ibid., 229.

Reed states[83] that the ABK members of the BUSA executive committee regarded with suspicion the long drawn-out uncertainty in connection with the policy.

The BUSA allowed associations to be in membership with it. These associations had representatives at the BUSA executive committee of which the ABK, BASA, and BMSA, as associations, were members. The ABK felt comfortable with this, as it would not have to join the territorial associations of the BUSA. The territorial associations, as the name suggests, required that churches in a particular province be affiliated with that territorial association which had representation on the BUSA executive board. As an ethnic and language association, the ABK desired to have its representation on the executive board of the BUSA and not through the territorial association. The ABK feared that joining the territorial association would be a threat to its existence, as the territorial associations would be wholly multi-racial. Reed[84] records that attempts were made to keep the status quo with respect to ABK representation on the Executive Committee of the BUSA, and these were eventually accepted by the BUSA Assembly.

Although it was accommodated on the executive committee, the ABK, as did the other associations, still maintained its identity. An interview with Dr. C. W. R. Lehmkuhl, the General Secretary of the ABK, on October 18, 2003, revealed that in 1996 the BUSA terminated the membership of associations within the BUSA. The BUSA had hoped that all ethnic and language associations would disband and that its churches would affiliate directly with the BUSA. The BUSA's rationale was that the BUSA was a union of Churches and not a union of associations.

The relationship of the ABK and the BUSA had high and low points. There were times when they differed. One example is when the BUSA applied for membership to the South African Council of Churches. The ABK, according to Hudson-Reed, considered this unacceptable. Only a limited number of ABK members attend the BUSA assembly meetings. Hudson-Reed hoped that both sides would take advantage of the current changing political climate to work for a greater degree of unity.[85]

---

83. Ibid., 230.
84. Ibid.
85. Ibid., 231.

The history of the Afrikaners in South Africa as recorded by Stack and Morton, Loubser, Davenport, de Gruchy, and Regehr,[86] reveals the pattern among Afrikaners in general as well as in the ABK at that time. The issue of race relations became an issue in the ABK. The BUSA raised this with the ABK in a protracted meeting held in 1960, and as mentioned earlier, the BUSA recommended to the ABK that it should form a separate Union.[87] Was that British imperialism or Afrikaner leaning towards apartheid? The response of BUSA to the government on several occasions where it opposed certain laws concerning the rights of Blacks suggests that the BUSA was serious about the issue of race relations, at least in words.

THE BCSA AND THE BUSA

William Mashologu is recorded as being the person who started the Baptist Convention of South Africa, formerly known as the Bantu Baptist Church. During his missionary activity in the Transkei, now called Eastern Cape, Mashologu recognized how fragmented Baptists in South Africa were.[88]

In the document "Proposal Concerning Promoting Reconciliation Between the Baptist Convention and the Baptist Union of South Africa," it was stated that one of the basic reasons for the present divisions between the BUSA and BCSA appears to be different perceptions of the past. This document goes on to qualify this statement. The BUSA has repeatedly claimed that it did not support apartheid. Indeed, it spoke out against apartheid. However, its perception of the BCSA's own structures as well as its failure to actively resist apartheid was questionable. Kretzschmar, as stated earlier, strongly supported the claim about the lack of practical commitment by the BUSA to oppose apartheid.

The Baptist World Alliance (BWA), under the leadership of its General Secretary Dr. Denton Lotz, captured other reasons for the disunity between the BUSA and the BCSA. He did this by gathering his leadership in the BWA to listen to the voices of both these organizations. This took place on November 18, 1995 at the Rosebank Union Church in Johannesburg. Lotz called it a "Listening Tour." On Thursday, November

---

86. Stack and Morton, *Torment to Triumph*, 26; Loubser, *Bible*, 5; Davenport, *South Africa*, 331; De Gruchy, *Struggle*, 54; Regehr, *Perceptions*, 103.

87. Hudson-Reed, *By Taking Heed*, 229.

88. Hoffmeister and Gurney, *Workshop*, 33.

16, 1995, he, together with his leadership, met separately with the BCSA and the following day with the BUSA. Each of the delegates of the BWA was required to summarize what he/she heard.

Their summaries reflected the same underlying misunderstanding of the past as was held by the two groups. Emmet Dunn, the youth director of the Baptist World Alliance, observed that the same story of the past was told but from different perspectives. He also stated that he was not sure if the younger generation understood the issues of the past. He warned that this division might produce two generations of fighting. This was echoed by Paul Montacute of the BWA, who went on to say that historical perceptions differ between the two organizations. Eleazar Ziherambere (BWA) admitted that the more he listened to the two sides, the less he understood the problem. He challenged the two organizations to work together.

Lotz, who acted as the facilitator at these talks, summarized their observations. The following themes surfaced during this "Listening Tour."

Merger: Revision versus New Vision

The BUSA and the BCSA did not succeed in an earlier attempt to reconcile. In 1987 the merger talks between these two organizations did not yield any results.

> The failure of the merger talks of 1987 revolves around the understanding of unity and the Constitution. Merger failed because one wanted a revision of the Constitution and the other wanted a new vision exemplified in a completely new constitution, not a re-write of the old one.[89]

History: Mission versus Submission

Whereas the Union viewed its history as a glorious story of mission to the unevangelized and non-Christian natives, the Convention viewed this history as one of submission. The natives suffered the indignities of being treated as children and inferiors, ruled by the White leaders with no power sharing.[90]

---

89. Rosebank Minutes, 3.
90. Ibid.

The Baptist Union's history as recorded by Hudson-Reed[91] does reflect a one-sided narrative in which the efforts of its pioneers and achievements of the BUSA's ministry are highlighted. This history is critically viewed by Kretzschmar,[92] and Hoffmeister.[93] They pointed out the suppression of knowledge of the plight of Black Baptists.

Theology: Evangelism versus Diakonia

In South Africa at that time, with its social, economic and political inequalities, it seemed that only the BCSA was serious about this state of affairs, which affected the everyday lives of Black Baptists. According to the observation made by Lotz's leadership, the difference in the theologies of the two organizations and how they contributed to the misunderstanding was as follows:

> There are two theologies at play between the two organizations which, according to him, is the main driving force that has caused much misunderstanding. The BUSA constantly speaks of church growth, evangelism and personal conversion. The BCSA speaks constantly of diakonia, service and justice.[94]

Theological Education: Indoctrination versus Contextualization

Theological education is an important area identified by Lotz and his leadership team:

> Training of pastors is a key to the future ministry of the church. Indoctrination versus contextualization may be a caricature of how the union and the convention do theological education, but it does highlight two different streams of structures of education. Whereas the BUSA has an elaborate system of theological colleges and Bible Schools, the BCSA is financially prevented from this. The BCSA theological courses are too Western and White and do not understand the contextual problems of the Blacks.[95]

---

91. Hudson-Reed, *By Taking Heed*, 15.
92. Hoffmeister and Gurney, *Workshop*, 30.
93. Ibid., 52–55.
94. Rosebank Minutes, 3.
95. Ibid.

I myself graduated from the Baptist Union Theological College and noticed the two different streams of theological education. Although some Blacks were allowed to study at their colleges, the colleges were largely designed for Whites, and they adopted a very restrictive theological framework. One's social and political context was generally ignored.

Leadership and the Unity Process: Evolution versus Revolution

The impatience of the BCSA was evident, and it seemed that the political developments in the country gave them the motivation and encouragement to pursue unity with the BUSA.

The Union leaders seem to be saying that it is inevitable that ten or fifteen union leaders will be Black, they will be the majority and they will rule. In a sense it will be a growing process, an evolutionary process. The BCSA leadership, on the other hand, is not prepared to wait. The secular government of Nelson Mandela assumed power in a peaceful revolution. What are Baptists waiting for?[96]

Repentance: Gospel versus Law

Since repentance is such a critical issue in the Bible, a biblical understanding of this is necessary.

It seemed that there was a difference of understanding. The BUSA feels that their resolution of repentance sent by the letter to the BCSA is enough of a sign of repentance and should be received with forgiveness by the BCSA. This is the Gospel way. The BCSA feels that the content of the repentance is not enough. There can be no cheap repentance. It needs to be the cross and suffering. It needs to mention specific acts of evil perpetuated by the BUSA, e.g., sending chaplains to minister to the other side of the border. What about specific instances where the intelligence forces used Baptists to report on activities of Black Baptists causing harm? What is the solution and what is the content of repentance? Is it "an eye for an eye" or is it "love your enemies."[97]

The BUSA's first step of sending the BCSA the aforementioned letter was a necessary one but does not measure up to genuine repentance. The BCSA's call for being specific is the next step so that the perpetrator and victim can find each other.

96. Rosebank Minutes, 1–3.
97. Ibid.

Lotz, being an outsider, demonstrated a high degree of objectivity, and his observations of the tensions, perceptions, and interpretations of issues by the BUSA and the BCSA were summarized very well. While the Awareness Workshop of the BCSA held in 1990 dealt with many of the issues summarized by Lotz, such as inferior theological education for Blacks, mission work by the BUSA to the Black churches, the structures of the BUSA and its understanding of repentance, Lotz is very specific in the areas that contrasted the polarized views, which had often been misportrayed or misunderstood by one side about the other. His thematic analysis of the differing views reflected by the two organizations were well presented.[98]

THE BASA AND THE BUSA

As mentioned earlier, there is not much available literature that reflects the history of BASA and highlights the relationship between these two organizations. According to Hudson-Reed,[99] formal contact with the BUSA is first referred to as having occurred in 1923. He also records the acceptance of Rev. T. M. Rangiah as a ministerial member of the Union. The BASA was accepted as a special association of BUSA and had representation on the executive committee of the BUSA. BASA had a good relationship with the SABMS, a missionary society of the BUSA through which BUSA sent a number of missionaries to work among the Indians in BASA and BMSA. When the BUSA changed its constitution to encourage special associations to affiliate with its territorial association and to request that churches within those special associations join the BUSA directly, two organizations opposed this: the ABK and the BASA. Then-BASA General Secretary V. P. Nathaniel, sent a letter to the BUSA outlining its objection. In summary BASA objected for the following reasons:

Fellowship and Interaction Among Baptists

Because of apartheid generally and the Group Areas Act of 1950 in particular, Indians have lived in Indian areas and have developed Baptist work in their own areas. The Group Areas Act provided for the setting aside of separate areas for business and residence for Indians, coloreds,

---

98. Rosebank Minutes, 1–8.
99. Hudson-Reed, *By Taking Heed*, 86.

The BASA and Unity Talks   95

blacks and whites.[100] Nathaniel[101] contended that the Act rendered fellowship and interaction impractical. He also cited the absence of white churches between Durban North and Empangeni (where most of the BASA churches are located) to further substantiate his contention.

Nathaniel stated that the cost of traveling to the executive meetings was another factor and that the building of churches was a higher priority. The executive meetings rotated among the various South African provinces.

In the event of disputes in churches, the arbitrators could be BASA, NBA, or the BUSA, or perhaps all three. Nathaniel expressed his fear that in the event of a split the aggrieved party had a ready haven in the BUSA. Indeed, such a pattern had developed.

Nathaniel stressed BASA's intentions to maintain its identity. Affiliation with the BUSA, he contended, would lead to dual allegiance. He belabored the point that BASA was of the opinion that dual allegiance would militate against the organizational norms, practices, and control so carefully nurtured since 1903.

BUSA/BASA Relations

Nathaniel[102] described an incident in 1992 that disappointed the BASA. The BUSA president and his wife were in Natal. Mr. N. M. Israel of BASA met them by coincidence and hastily arranged a tour of BASA churches the following day. A car was provided to take them to Kearsney and the Bible College on the Natal North Coast. They covered seven churches and 400 kilometers in five hours. The next day, at the BASA Easter assembly, the President brought greetings and mentioned with appreciation the trip and history of each church related by Mr. N. M. Israel. Two months later, at the BUSA Annual Assembly, a BASA representative gave the president an album of photographs of the trip. In the BUSA's presidential report to the executive, he reported on his visit to the Western Province churches but there was not a single word about the Indian experience.

Nathaniel registered further concern and disappointment that the president of the Baptist Women's Department of BUSA, who was invited to a rally by the Women's Department of BASA, reported to her executive committee very little about the BASA women's rally at which she was a

100. Palmer, *History*, 142.
101. Nathaniel, Letter, 2.
102. Ibid., 3.

guest speaker. In addition, the BASA youth department was sending its newsletter "Youth Update" to the Youth Department of BUSA, but no communication regarding their youth work was shared with BASA youth.

Nathaniel drew the BUSA's attention to the recording of minutes of BASA's representative to the BUSA executive. N. M. Israel, at the March executive meeting of BUSA, held in Claremont, shared the history of Indian Baptist work in South Africa as well as the split that occurred, resulting in the formation of BASA and the BMSA. The minutes read, "Mr. N. M. Israel addressed the executive committee on some historical details of the split between two Indian groups in Natal."[103] Fortunately, at that meeting no representative from the BMSA was present; otherwise those minutes would have caused problems had they been read by non-executive members.

It is apparent that BASA has been aggrieved by the attitude and actions of the BUSA. The reasons given by Nathaniel[104] are not obstacles to unity; instead they are obstacles to closer cooperation and, more so, obstacles to affiliation with the Natal Baptist Association, which, as mentioned earlier, is the territorial association of BUSA. Presently BASA has no representation on the BUSA executive committee or on its territorial association, though it has a cordial relationship with BUSA.

The BMSA and the BUSA

The Baptist Mission of South Africa (BMSA) is the smallest of the five Baptist organizations in South Africa. It has thirteen churches with a combined membership of approximately 1500.[105]

On July 29, 1951, the BMSA executive committee decided to join the BUSA. By the decision of 1951, the general assembly of the BUSA accepted the BMSA as a member church. This implied that the BMSA enjoyed the privilege of having the liberty to carry on with its own work.

Hudson-Reed[106] writes that later, in 1974, the BMSA applied for association status with the BUSA, but that this was unsuccessful. Some of the BMSA churches—such as Arena Park Baptist Church, Asherville Baptist Church and Bethel Baptist Church in Stanger—affiliated directly with the

---

103. Ibid.
104. Ibid., 4.
105. Baptist World Alliance.
106. Hudson-Reed, *By Taking Heed*, 276.

BUSA. Although the BMSA was not accepted as an association within the structures of BUSA, it was represented on the BUSA executive committee.[107]

BASA's Response to Racism and Apartheid

BASA's response to the idea of a united Baptist organization in South Africa must be viewed primarily in light of its response to apartheid and racism. In 1964, the South African government established the National Indian Council, which enforced the Indian identity along the lines of separate development.[108] Then in the mid-1980s the National Party continued with its racial policies by introducing a system of government that included Indians by allowing them limited political power. This system of government, which allowed Indians and Coloreds limited political power, was called the tri-cameral parliament. It consisted of three houses of chamber: the House of Assembly for Whites, House of Representatives for Coloreds, and the House of Delegates for Indians.

By 1993 most of the House of Delegates members supported the National Party.[109] When an election was held to elect members to the House of Delegates, only 20.3 percent of the Indian community went to the polls.[110] Although this was a low turnout for this election, a pattern developed among Indian voting in the 1994 and 1999 elections. In both these elections, 60 percent of Indians voted for the National Party.[111] It seemed that despite the oppressive ideology of the National Party, the majority of Indians did not make a break from its ethnic orientation. The National Party provided a system through its separate development policy that promoted the Indian propensity towards ethnicity. None of the BASA leaders or members publicly supported liberation movements such as the Natal Indian Congress, African National Congress, United Democratic Front, Azanian Peoples Organization, and the Pan African Congress. Some significant members of the Indian community, including Strini Moodley, Jay Naidoo, Saths Cooper, Mac Maharaj, Pravin Gordan, and Frene Ginwala, did not support the House of Delegates. These leaders warned the Indian community against participating in the

---

107. Ibid.
108. Dhupelia-Mesthrie, *From Fields to Freedom*, 24.
109. Ibid.
110. Ibid., 25.
111. Ibid., 27.

tri-cameral elections. The NIBA News, which was written by M. Rangiah, great grandson of John Rangiah, does not make reference to racism and apartheid in its survey of the missionary enterprise of the Natal Indian Baptist Association from 1903 to 1953.[112]

Although Timothy[113] wrote about the Group Areas Act and its effect on the Indian community (resulting in the Indians being removed from Cato Manor, North Street in Durban and being resettled in Chatsworth and Phoenix), BASA has been largely silent on the issue of racism and apartheid.

DIVISION IN THE INDIAN BAPTIST WORK IN SOUTH AFRICA

Indian Baptists in South Africa once belonged to the Telugu Indian Baptist Mission Church. John Rangiah founded the Telugu Indian Baptist Church, but the years 1911 to 1914 saw the Indian Baptist work go through difficult times. Division among Indian Baptists surfaced. M. Rangiah, editor of the *Natal Indian Baptist Association Brochure*, describes this division:

> Rev. Rangiah preached a sermon on sin and its results and this was interpreted as excommunication by the dissentient group. The group then persuaded a few others to join it and wrote without Rev. Rangiah's knowledge, to the Home Missionary Society (HMS) in India. Rangiah was disappointed that he was not informed of this decision to write to the HMS in India and that the proper channels were not followed. After meeting with Rev. W. B. Boggs who was sent by the HMS in India to settle the dispute, Rev. Rangiah resigned from the HMS. Rev. Boggs returned to India without success in settling the dispute."[114]

T. Paul, in his research on Pentecostalism among the Indian churches in the Stanger area, records this schism between the two organizations.[115] According to Paul,[116] the reasons are similar to the one in the NIBA Golden Jubilee of 1964, except that Paul gave the following information that was not contained in the above publication. He stated that a group of aggrieved members sent a petition to the TBHMS accusing the missionary of living a sumptuous life at the expense of the laborers and of making

---

112. Rangiah *NIBA News*, 1–57.
113. Timothy, *Risecliff*, 7.
114. Rangiah, *Brochure*, 10.
115. Paul, "Pentecostal Churches," 4–5.
116. Ibid.

efforts to sever his connection with the HMS in India. These accusations do not appear in any of the minutes of the BASA and the BMSA.

Neither of these records is specific with regard to the differences. Rev. T. D. Pass, a BUSA missionary to the Indian Baptists, is quoted in the *Diamond Jubilee* brochure[117] as saying, "Explaining the causes of the rift between Rev. Rangiah and the group now called the Indian Baptist Mission is difficult since only BASA has offered any explanation and not with enough detail to permit evaluation and judgment." He continued, "It may be that the real roots lie below the surface and their germination in relationship between various parties before they left India." To date, neither the BASA nor the BMSA are able to specifically state the reasons for the schism.

Whatever the reasons for the schism that took place between 1911 and 1914 in which the BASA and BMSA parted ways, there have been attempts to amalgamate it, though without success. In assessing these attempts, not many leaders, especially in BASA, have explored a theological basis for unity. One exception is the late Rev. D. N. Nathaniel, an Indian-born minister who, as noted earlier, arrived in South Africa in 1951 and served the BASA until his death in the late 1980s. In his research he provides a theological basis for unity by making references to Scripture, citing, among other things, Jesus' prayer for unity in John 17:21. He goes on to state: "As we strive to achieve Church union under an appropriate title it would be right and proper if we eliminate selfish and divergent views."

MOVEMENT TOWARDS UNITY

The political change in South Africa provided BASA with an opportunity to engage other Baptists in the pursuit of unity. We now turn to the various consultations and meetings of the five Baptist organizations that evidenced a desire to move towards unity.

The new political dispensation in South Africa in 1994 and the meeting of the Baptist World Alliance in Durban, South Africa in July of 1998 were turning points. Leading figures such as Rev. Desmond Hoffmeister of the BCSA initiated discussions with BASA and BMSA that took place at the Springfield College of Education in Durban in 1997. Another significant consultation between the BCSA and the BUSA took place in

---

117. Moses, *Diamond Jubilee*, 2.

Colesberg in 1998. These bilateral consultations between and among the various groups were a positive sign.

A major breakthrough came about when the Baptist World Alliance held its General Council meetings in Durban in 1998 at the invitation of the BUSA and the BCSA. This was the first time the BWA met in South Africa. It had not done so previously because of its strong opposition to apartheid.

Rev. Hoffmeister, General Secretary of the BCSA, requested that the BWA include other Baptists in South Africa as part of the Local Arrangements Committee (LAC) for the BWA. During this General Council meeting, Terry Rae, the General Secretary of the BUSA, said: "We need to sit down and talk to each other." It was decided at that General Council meeting by the leaders of the South African Baptist organizations—Reverends Hoffmeister (BCSA) and Rae (BUSA); Mr. Dan Philip (BMSA); President of the BASA Anthony Poliah; and I (as Vice-President of BASA and chair of the LAC) that we would begin a process of dialogue.

For the first time in the history of Baptists, a multi-racial Baptist committee was established to work together in organizing the logistics for the arrival of the General Council delegates of the BWA. Despite certain challenges, one of which was the resignation of the secretary (a member of the BUSA) of the LAC at the first formal meeting of this committee, the General Council Meeting was a huge success.[118]

The work of the South African Baptists (particularly in the LAC) paved the way for Baptists to move towards cooperation. The formation of the South African Baptist Alliance was a result of the cooperative efforts of the five Baptist organizations in South Africa.

---

118. Ragwan, *In His Service*, 63.

8

The BASA and the South African Baptist Alliance

After a successful General Council meeting in Durban, the Local Arrangements Committee (LAC) expressed the desire to meet to explore unity among Baptists in South Africa. From 1999 to 2003, the LAC held several meetings to discuss this possibility.

THE SPRINGFIELD CONSULTATION

The Springfield Consultation took place as a result of conversations between Rev. Hoffmeister and myself in 1997. I wrote at the time that Hoffmeister, in his foresight, saw the bigger picture as it applied to Baptist cooperation and unity. He wanted to meet with the leadership of BASA. It was the first time the BASA leadership was to meet a Black leader from the BCSA. Hoffmeister also extended the invitation to the BMSA. In April of 1997 the three Baptist organizations—BCSA, BASA and BMSA—met in Springfield, Durban to discuss cooperation. The three organizations resolved to engage one another in working towards unity. As previously noted, this began to happen during planning for the General Council of the BWA in July of 1998.[1]

THE COLESBERG CONSULTATION

This historic consultation took place between the BUSA and BCSA at Colesberg on May 14 and 15, 1998. It was facilitated by Dr. Ruben

1. Ragwan, *In His Service*, 62.

Richards at the request and invitation of the two General Secretaries of the BCSA and the BUSA. Dr. Richards served as the executive secretary of the Truth and Reconciliation Commission (TRC).[2] He outlined the government's TRC process with specific emphasis on its purpose, which, he stated, was to deal with the past and the abuses of human rights, as well as to develop a mechanism to provide procedures to restore the damages done in the past. He went on to state that contrition, confession, and forgiveness were necessary for healing to take place. He drew the attention of the delegates at Colesberg to the need for Baptists to acknowledge that crimes had been committed in the name of Christianity and that it would be necessary for Baptists not only to have a shared memory of the past but to be accountable as well. Against this background both the organizations were given opportunities to share both their hurts and concerns.[3]

According to the minutes,[4] representatives from each group shared their views regarding hurts and concerns. They ranged from name calling to confiscation of property. I will provide more details later. For now, suffice it to say that the Colesberg meeting was key to getting the two organizations to deal with the past so that unification could take center stage in future talks.

THE BULWER ROAD CONSULTATION

The first multi-racial Baptist forum was held on February 19, 1999 at the Bulwer Road Baptist Church in Durban. The BCSA was represented by the Rev. D. Hoffmeister, Rev. M. J. Sibiya, Rev. L. Jacob, Rev. S. Dlamini, Rev. P. Sibiya, Rev. Anzima, Rev. A Dlamini, Rev. S. A. Khanyile and Rev. D. J. Mashiga. The BUSA was represented by Rev. T. Rae, Rev. B. E. Mcambi, Rev. A. Sibiya and Rev. G.M. Ngamlana. The BMSA's delegates were Mr. D. Philip, Rev. L. Benjamin and Rev. J. Moses. BASA was represented by Mr. N. M. Israel, Mrs. R. Israel, Mr. A. Poliah, Pastor R. Nathaniel, Mrs. F. Nathaniel, and myself. At this stage the ABK was not part of the forum, though it joined later.[5]

This forum allowed each organization to share its vision for Baptists in South Africa. All delegates committed themselves to reconciliation

---

2. Colesberg Minutes, 9–12.
3. Ibid.
4. Ibid.
5. Baptist Unity in South Africa minutes, 12 (1999).

and unity. A proposal[6] to elect a committee to work toward continued reconciliation and cooperation among all Baptists in South Africa and to bring the others into the ongoing national process of reconciliation was adopted unanimously. The committee was comprised of:

BUSA—Rev. Terry Rae
BCSA—Rev. Desmond Hoffmeister
BASA—Rev. Rodney Ragwan
BMSA—Mr. Daniel Philip

Revs. Dan Cole of the American Baptist Churches, USA and Dwight Reagan of the Southern Baptist Convention, USA were elected facilitators. The function of the above committee was to develop a resolution for a way forward and to establish the next meeting time for the dialogue to continue. The first meeting of this forum was a positive sign that Baptists were at last willing to talk to one another.

It was apparent that the BUSA, BCSA, BMSA and BMSA were willing to begin a new chapter in Baptist relations in South Africa. Terry Rae, the General Secretary of the BUSA, expressed[7] the need for efforts towards building a stronger Baptist family in the Kwa Zulu region. Hoffmeister, the General Secretary of the BCSA, also expressed the need to work together. He stated that Baptists must develop a joint vision using "us and us" rather than "we and them."[8] He urged members to embrace a "bottom up" approach to reconciliation. The BMSA's Daniel Philip committed his organization to structural unity among Baptists.[9] BASA as well as BMSA expressed regret for working only with the Indian community in Kwa Zulu Natal.[10] This constituted a shift in thinking by BASA from wanting to remain an ethnic organization to embracing other racial groups.[11]

The second meeting[12] of this forum was held on April 9, 1999 at Bulwer Road Baptist Church. It was convened and facilitated by Rev.

---

6. Ibid.
7. Ibid., 19.
8. Ibid., 13.
9. Ibid.
10. Ibid., 12.
11. Nathaniel, letter, 2.
12. BRBM Minutes, 16.

Dan Cole, a missionary of the American Baptist Churches, USA. At this second meeting a "Memorandum of Understanding" was formulated. It gave a name to the forum: The South African Baptist Alliance (SABA). Its purpose, objectives, and governing principles were discussed and finalized. The purpose as recorded in the memorandum stated:

> The purpose is to strengthen the Baptist witness and cooperate in ministry with each body remaining autonomous. The business of the Baptist bodies of the Alliance shall be facilitated by a coordinating executive comprising between two and four representatives from each group.[13]

In response to the purpose stated in the "Memorandum of Understanding," the following statements were made by each organization:[14]

BUSA stated that this process should bring about perfect unity such as discussed in 1 Corinthians 1:10.

BCSA stated that it was open to this process and that a resolution was made at its Easter Conference in 1999 affirming the need for reconciliation, fellowship, and unity.

BMSA stated that there must be an unconditional commitment as suggested in Ephesians 4:1–5.

BASA stated that the walls that separated Baptists needed to be broken down. There was a need for delegates to consider the love of Christ in order to become one as Christ and the Father are one, as stated in Ephesians 2:14.

After a time of prayer there was a discussion of barriers in the relationships among Baptist organizations. The barriers cited are as follows:

1. Lack of communication between Baptist groups;
2. Tone of communication;
3. Constitution that is inflexible and without representation;
4. Power struggle for dominance;
5. Ignorance of each other's history, hopes and character;
6. Access to the international Baptist family.[15]

For the first time these organizations were able to openly express how these barriers impeded their desire to cooperate. The list of barriers

---

13. "Memorandum of Understanding," Durban, 9 March 1999.
14. Bulwer Road Minutes, 16.
15. BRBM Minutes, 17.

made it clear that there were deficiencies in the amount of and the tone of communication among Baptists. The issue of the constitution applied to the BUSA, as the other organizations felt the BUSA's constitution was inflexible and non-representative. Even when it was amended to make room for others, it was done in a way that required others to either join on BUSA's terms or risk being left out of its structures. Prior to the changing of the BUSA constitution, BASA, BMSA, and the ABK were considered affiliate organizations of the BUSA, in which they had limited representation on its executive council only.[16]

Baptists were to a large extent ignorant of one another's history, hopes, and character. Delegates from the non-BUSA organizations expressed concern that the BUSA did not recognize the rich history and valuable contributions that BASA, BMSA, and BCSA had made to Christian witness in South Africa.[17]

Another barrier was racism.[18] It would be naïve to think that, given the socio-political conditions in the country and the racial composition of the five Baptist organizations, that racism had disappeared.

The facilitator engaged each of the organizations, urging them to discuss their visions for how these barriers might be overcome in order to provide a way forward. Delegates expressed the hope that there would be free communication with open language between and among leaders and members of the five organizations, communication characterized by love and respect for others and for their respective organizations. It was hoped that a constitution, especially of BUSA, would be open to all voices. The issue of racism received attention as well, and it was resolved that each organization work towards eradicating this barrier both within individuals as well as in the structures of the five organizations.[19]

It was further decided that to overcome the problem of ignorance, unity and reconciliation meetings would be held and pulpit exchange and fellowship among congregations of the various organizations would be encouraged. These efforts, according to the delegates, would provide opportunities for the members to appreciate the richness of their diversity.

16. Ibid.
17. Ibid.
18. Ibid.
19. Ibid.

It was decided that a mechanism needed to be put into place to move the organizations closer to the goal of unity. This mechanism would include:

1. Confession, in which participants accept their responsibilities and own what they have done;
2. Restitution and fulfilment of obligations;
3. Recognition of particular conflicts that require intervention.[20]

The BCSA on April 9, 1999 went on to propose the establishment of a cooperative body of Baptists in South Africa. According to the BCSA, this would encourage cooperation and open communication and create a forum to deal with conflicts and unresolved issues from the past. The BCSA added that this body could be expanded to include other Baptist bodies and to look at wider issues such as social inequalities, leadership, and community development in the country.

As the Baptist organization that was viewed with suspicion over the years by most of the other Baptist organizations, the following statement from the BUSA was very significant:

> We acknowledge that in the past, we as the BUSA, have acted wrongfully and sinfully towards Baptist bodies in South Africa who were historically represented at a leadership level in our denomination. We confess as sinful our exclusionary mindset, our constitutional inflexibility, our lack of proper communication, as well as a deep-seated ignorance. We also confess that there have been times when co-operation did take place and we did not give proper acknowledgement or show adequate respect to smaller bodies. We have demonstrated a pattern of not noting the co-operation, growth and development of smaller Baptist bodies. We acknowledge that this has caused deep hurt and division in the past for which we are deeply sorry and we trust you will grant us forgiveness. In order to prevent this from happening again and to move forward together we propose that delegations from the four Baptist bodies meet every six months for the purpose of communication, co-operation and unity. The goal is to engage each other so that we can ultimately become one Baptist body in South Africa.[21]

The BMSA, a predominantly Indian organization, made the following statement:

---

20. Ibid., 17–18.
21. Ibid., 3.

The Mission confesses to many wrong doings for the way we treated each other because of the laws of our country. Our present ideals are to see restored relationships and to have some form of combined fellowship. Ultimately the Baptist Mission is committed to one Baptist body. In order for this to come about we suggest the formation of a facilitating committee, with each body having equal representation. We express the need to have one voice. Baptist Mission will take every initiative to Baptist unity. We will not commit ourselves to any process but Baptist unity. We need to have a neutral facilitator. We need to look at other denominations that have had a unification process, for help. We must adhere to the principles of honesty and transparency. Today is the beginning of a great day in our lives.[22]

The strong call for unity from the BMSA was a result of its own consultation that took place in Deep River, Kwa Zulu Natal, February 5–7, 1993. At this Deep River Consultation, sixty delegates from the churches of the BMSA mapped out a vision for the future. They spent three days formulating a mission statement, outlining objectives, making confession, recognizing the challenges for the future relationships among their churches and other Baptist denominations, and developing strategies and a commitment to action. One of its objectives, as stated in its covenant, was to "promote unity and brotherly love among churches of the mission and association within the mission." It also committed itself to unification of the Baptist denomination, and noted the fragmentation of the polarized state of the church in South Africa.[23]

The statement made by BASA, a largely ethnic organization, was summarized in the minutes as acknowledging the need to work together and to go beyond their hurt. They said that in their ignorance they had hurt others. They regretted past actions that caused hurt. They also said that they submitted to the cleansing of the precious blood of Jesus and wished to move with a new spirit of fellowship.[24]

Each of the organizations' statements embodied confession and regret of past actions. There was optimism that this process would proceed to the next level. That next level, as recorded[25] in the April 9, 1999 minutes

22. BRBM Minutes, 4.
23. Daniel, *Deep River*, 2.
24. BRBM Minutes, 4.
25. Ibid., 12–14.

of BUSA, was the discussion of the model for a Baptist forum in South Africa. A suggested name, South African Baptist Alliance (SABA), was received positively. SABA would comprise the four groups, which would engage one another regularly and work towards unity. It was also suggested that issues such as racism, tribalism, suspicion, and resources be dealt with by this forum. Delegates shared some of the challenges of a "top down" approach, which required a person of passion to drive the process.

A groundbreaking resolution was put together by a special committee of this forum. It read:

> We, the delegates of the Baptist Convention of South Africa, the Baptist Association of South Africa, the Baptist Mission of South Africa and the Baptist Union of Southern Africa, on this 9th day April of 1999, in order to explore reconciliation, forgiveness and unity among our constituent bodies experienced the guidance and conviction of the Holy Spirit as we expressed our past, our hurts, our divisions and our sins. A time of introspection led us to identify barriers to unite. We have acknowledged the move of God in our midst, which led us to express our hopes for the future and our common desire for a single united Baptist body in South Africa. We have resolved to take this report back to our executives for discussion and for them to appoint delegates to continue deliberation on the 2nd of July 1999.[26]

The resolution was approved unanimously. It was then determined that each body would take the results of this meeting to its executives and appoint four persons to meet on July 2, 1999 at the Bulwer Road Baptist Church to continue the process, as stated in the last statement of the resolution. Delegates participated in a "Communion Service" with prayer offered for the process.

THE KEMPTON PARK CONSULTATION

The third meeting was held on March 31, 2000 at the ABK Seminary in Kempton Park, Johannesburg. The minutes recorded the participation of the Afrikaanse Baptiste Kerk at the Baptist Forum. At the outset the General Secretary, Dr. Carl Lehmkuhl, in greeting the group, stated that the ABK was willing and prepared to work with the four groups.[27]

---

26. Ibid., 5.
27. Kempton Park Minutes, 9.

The resolution that was accepted by the SABA executive committee had to be discussed by the respective executive committees of the five Baptist organizations and was to be reported on at the next meeting. The responses of the five organizations after consulting with their respective executive committees were as follows:

ABK accepted the proposal and was willing and prepared to work together with the Alliance. BCSA suggested that due to the prevailing problems and misunderstanding in both the BCSA and the BUSA constituencies, energies and efforts should be focused on relationship building and reconciliation, first at the grassroots level and then on other levels. It further suggested that cooperation be sought among the five Baptist bodies in South Africa in such areas as theological education, ministers and staff pension fund, and mission so as to enhance a common Baptist witness in South Africa.

BUSA reported that its executive committee felt the resolution was too broad. Representatives felt that there was work to do specifically in the area of what the forum was going to consider with regard to theological education. It was further reported that there would be no vote on the resolution until it was concrete and specific in this area. BMSA stated that it was interested in the process but would prefer to see some time frame as well as an evaluation process put in place. BASA reported that its executive committee was generally in favor of the process but was waiting for specifics.

The facilitator, Rev. Dan Cole, was recorded to have said at this meeting that the group had to take ownership of this process. He recommended that each of the Baptist organizations select one person to a committee of conveners. These five would become conveners for future meetings of the Alliance. Cole suggested that these conveners rotate in the beginning; in this way delegates would learn to appreciate the leadership style of each group. The conveners selected by the five organizations were P. Msiza (BCSA), T. Rae (BUSA), C. Lehmkuhl (ABK), D. Philip or B. Naidoo (BMSA) and myself (BASA). The conveners were given a suggested agenda for future meetings with the objective of cooperating as Baptists in South Africa.

THE ARENA PARK CONSULTATION

The fourth meeting was held on August 18, 2000 at Arena Park Baptist Church in Chatsworth, Durban. This meeting[28] began with a proposal of a statement by the BU. Rev. Terry Rae of the BUSA proposed the following mission statement:

The purpose of the South African Baptist Alliance is to strengthen the Baptist witness in South Africa by vesting a forum where the participating bodies may forge a closer fellowship, discuss matters of common concern, speak with a united voice and develop a co-operative ministry.[29]

This statement seemed a little watered down from its statement at the first consultation in Durban, which stated[30] that there was a need for a strong Baptist witness in Kwa Zulu Natal. Then in the second consultation it referenced 1 Corinthians 1:10. The BUSA challenged the members to dare to risk for God.[31] However, the statement proposed at the third consultation[32] did not contain the strong call for unity. Instead it proposed that Baptists work together. It was, nevertheless, accepted by members of SABA.

THE PRIORITY OF PRAYER

Prayer has been a strong focus of the SABA. At each executive meeting, time is taken for each organization to report on its activities after which time has been allocated to pray for one another and for the activities of each of the five organizations. These are recorded in the minutes of the SABA meetings.

Despite calls from delegates in the respective organizations for their newsletters and brochures to include the progress, activities, and the discussions of the five Baptist organizations, has not been a successful function of SABA. It was reported, however, at a meeting at the Durban North Baptist Church on June 15, 2001 that the BUSA would advertise the official launch of SABA in its national brochure, *Baptist Today*. Terry Rae was recorded as saying that he would request the editor of *Baptist*

---

28. SABA Minutes 2000, 1–5.
29. BRBM Minutes, 1.
30. Ibid., 12.
31. Ibid., 16.
32. Kempton Park Minutes, 9.

Today to put together a brochure on the event that could be circulated to all Baptists in South Africa.[33]

SABA delegates stated that this forum would not have a constitution. Each organization, according to the minutes of the meeting of August 18, 2000 at the Arena Park Baptist Church, Chatsworth, stated that the Alliance would follow a simple structure of fellowship with each organization remaining autonomous and that a coordinating executive council would be formed to facilitate fellowship and cooperation. It was also recorded that this executive committee would include between two and four representatives from each group.[34]

COOPERATION IN MINISTRY

The following ministry projects were listed as possible ways the five organizations could cooperate: theological education, missions, church planting, disaster relief, and community projects such as HIV/AIDS. Only two of these areas have enjoyed the cooperation of the five organizations. One was theological education. The All Africa Baptist Fellowship (AABF), a regional organization of the BWA, held a Theological Educators Conference in Johannesburg at the Honey Dew Conference Center on June 24–27, 2003. SABA elected a committee to arrange this conference on behalf of AABF. Delegates from three of the five Baptist organizations participated.[35]

The other significant cooperative ministry in which all five Baptist organizations participated was the X-treme team ministry. This ministry was a youth program of the American Baptist Churches, USA that allowed individuals to experience Christian ministry in different cultural and geographical locations around the world. Representatives from the five bodies traveled to the U.S. to participate in this ministry from June 30 to August 9, 2003.[36]

Thus far there has not been any cooperation in church planting and community projects. Despite this, the five organizations committed themselves to pursuing ways of cooperating, including in the area of sharing principles of leadership.

33. SABA Minutes 2001, 2–4.
34. SABA Minutes 2002, 2.
35. SABA Minutes: 2003, 2.
36. Ibid.

The minutes recorded the concerns of the BUSA regarding the tensions between congregational and leadership models of church leadership. According to the BUSA, there was too much organizational leadership as compared to spiritual leadership. The other four Baptist organizations identified with this observation and requested that these trends be examined against international trends. This examination, however, was not done by the SABA.[37] Nor was any effort undertaken to compile a roll of pastors within the five organizations. The need for Christian schools appeared only once on the agenda. Discussions took place, but no real progress was made in this area.

PUBLIC RELATIONS

Rev. Terry Rae of the BUSA was elected the first facilitator of SABA in 2001.[38] The following year I was elected as SABA's facilitator. The main persons responsible for creating awareness of SABA and its objectives were supposed to be the general secretaries of the five organizations.

In the past BUSA addressed the government on certain issues, one of which was of a political nature, that is, the government's proposal to deprive Africans of their limited parliamentary representation. The BUSA condemned this proposal.[39] Although the present government meets with religious leaders from time to time, SABA does not have an official voice at this religious forum nor has it attempted to get such a voice.

A UNIFIED THEOLOGICAL COLLEGE

At the SABA meeting held at Arena Park Baptist Church in Chatsworth, Durban, the minutes recorded a discussion to unify the theological colleges of the ABK, BCSA, and the BUSA. Participants decided to hold a meeting of all three colleges. Those present viewed this in a positive light and hoped it would result in the merging of seminary programs and sharing of resources and personnel. It was hoped that this new institution would be a truly African Seminary where different languages and cultural backgrounds would be considered. Although BASA and BMSA did not

---

37. SABA Minutes 2000, 3.
38. SABA Minutes 2001, 1.
39. De Gruchy, *Struggle*, 54.

have established theological institutions, their representation and input were requested as well.[40]

There have been several meetings of the theological education committee during this period regarding the forming of a single Baptist theological college. Issues of concern to the main Baptist organizations included assets, resources, administration, salaries, legal implications, and theology. The minutes of October 31, 2003[41] recorded that the concept of a federal Baptist college in South Africa was desirable but not practical.

The main reason given by the BUSA was that its theological institution is accredited with the education department of the state while the ABK and the BCSA colleges were not. Furthermore, according to its General Secretary, the state would not consider the concept of three colleges on one campus. The other reason cited by the BUSA was administration, which for the BUSA would be, in the words of the new General Secretary, Angelo Scheepers, "a nightmare." Also, there would be differences in salaries for the various college faculties.

The concluding remarks, as recorded in the minutes, were that the BUSA felt the "time is not right" for such a concept. The other SABA delegates expressed disappointment at the failure of the concept of a federal Baptist college in South Africa. It was hoped that this united effort by SABA would be a significant development in the unification of the five Baptist organizations.[42] Failure by SABA to have a truly united institution where there would be three colleges sharing one campus demonstrated a lack of will by the BUSA to follow through with this concept.

As mentioned earlier, the BWA's presence in South Africa in July of 1998 had a very positive influence on Baptists. It resulted in the formation of the SABA. The meeting of the four Baptist organizations at Bulwer Road Baptist Church on February 19, 1999 must be considered a major breakthrough given the fragmented and polarized state of Baptists in South Africa. What is also significant is that the four groups extended an invitation to the ABK, an Afrikaner group, thus making the opportunity to join the process of unification an inclusive one. This was the first

---

40. SABA Minutes 2000, 2.
41. SABA minutes 2003, 2.
42. Ibid.

time in the history of BASA where it participated in a national forum that included the four main Baptist organizations.

The minutes of the Bulwer Road meeting recorded a proposal:

> Each body would take the results of this meeting to their executive councils and appoint 4 persons to meet…to continue this process.[43]

The four persons from each organization were tasked with facilitating reconciliation and cooperation among all Baptists in Kwa Zulu Natal and with bringing other Baptist organizations into the ongoing national process of reconciliation and unification. This can be regarded as a breakthrough given the non-cooperation of the five organizations in the past. However, Baptists had to come to terms with the past in order to move into the future. The BASA made a statement for these hurts to be dealt with.[44]

DEALING WITH THE PAST

The delegates agreed that before a merger could take place, a "Colesberg" type meeting was necessary. The delegates[45] agreed to this proposal: "… *the next meeting should include all Baptists by invitation to deal with past hurts.*" The proposal to create a forum to deal with past hurts was a step in the right direction in light of the Scriptural basis for confession and forgiveness.

The dawning in 1994 of a democratic country gave hope to Black people. BCSA, which represented Black Baptists, had suffered greatly under apartheid. It was important for them to share with other Baptists the hurts and obstacles of the past so that these would never be repeated. This starting point was important and necessary. BASA and BMSA also felt that such a forum was needed, that past hurts must be brought out into the open and dealt with. There needed to be confession and repentance for true healing to take place.

In a process such as this there are several challenges to consider. First, therehas been a lack of communication among Baptist organizations. Occasionally areas of concern were communicated by BASA and BCSA to the BUSA. However, responses to these concerns were not acknowledged by BUSA. The tone of the communications, especially between BUSA and BCSA, has often not been good.

43. Bulwer Road Minutes, 6.
44. BRBM Minutes, 16.
45. Ibid., 3.

A second obstacle is the BUSA constitution, which is inflexible. When the BUSA changed its constitution from a union of associations to a union of churches, it left the other organizations outside of the greater Baptist family, alienating the leaders who represented their respective organizations at the BUSA executive meetings.

Another barrier was the BUSA's treatment of the history of the BASA, BMSA, and the BCSA. Very little of this history appears in its publications and newsletters. The contributions of men and women in the history of these organizations are often ignored or not acknowledged. The BUSA specifically admitted in its statement that there had been times when cooperation did take place but that it did not give proper acknowledgement or show adequate respect by noting the cooperation, growth, and development of smaller Baptist organizations. At the first meeting of the four Baptist organizations on February 19, there was recognition that apartheid played a part in perpetuating five separate Baptist organizations; the five organizations participated in a time of confession and repentance similar to South Africa's Truth and Reconciliation Commission.[46]

The "Memorandum of Understanding" specifically defined SABA as a fellowship of bodies and asserted that each organization would remain autonomous. It reflected a lack of commitment of each organization except the BMSA to a new united Baptist organization in South Africa. This should not be misunderstood as reluctance by the other organizations to the idea of cooperation and working together in ministry. It simply means that there were many issues at stake in the event of creating a new united Baptist organization in South Africa, such as assets, resources, theological differences, tradition, and culture. It seemed that these were too costly a sacrifice to make. At the SABA meetings there were mostly young leaders from the five Baptist organizations. Not all of them were part of resolutions that were made by BUSA in the apartheid days, resolutions that had brought about hurt. Despite this, each organization confessed its wrongs and apologized for past actions. Each delegate participated in a concluding Holy Communion service.

The important element of restitution at this forum was absent. Given the enormous damage apartheid had caused and through which two organizations, BUSA and ABK, benefited, including in the areas of economics and education, no commitment was made to any kind of restitution.

46. Baptist Unity, 1.

Embracing such a principle would be huge and costly, but engaging in such a process, however small, would have been helpful symbolically.

Each of the Baptist organizations reflected in their statements at the first meeting in 1999 an openness to the idea of eventual unification. The leaders who sat around the SABA table were mostly important and influential officers in their respective organizations. When the principles and objectives of SABA were reported at their respective constituencies they were received positively. However, most of these constituencies called for more specific details. One example was recorded in the SABA minutes of a meeting held on March 31, 2000 in Kempton Park, Johannesburg, where the BUSA responded to the area of theological education. One has to bear in mind that Baptists also have variations in their theologies. The BUSA and ABK hold to a conservative evangelical theology with strong emphasis on evangelism and missions, while BCSA tends to be strong on contextual theology with a concern for both spiritual and social needs. BASA and BMSA tend to be positioned in the middle with a tendency at times to lean more towards conservatism.

The failure of SABA to pursue a federal Baptist college was a result of difficulties in areas of staffing, salaries, legal implications in regards to assets, property and administration. No mention was made of the curriculum. One is tempted to think that the issue of theology may have been a stumbling block in this process. The statements in the SABA meetings reflect the theological differences of the two main organizations, namely the BUSA and the BCSA. One is considered to be somewhat liberal and the other conservative. Many conservative evangelicals are not comfortable with liberation theology, which attempts to unite theology and socio-political concerns.[47]

On the other hand, Blacks from the BCSA as well as representatives of the two ethnically based organizations, BASA and BMSA, would argue that the conservative evangelicals from the BUSA and ABK, with their strong emphasis on evangelism and church planting, tend to be less concerned with the social issues facing the population of South Africa.

Another flaw in the unification process as set out in SABA was that the principles and objectives were not reaching the people on the ground. Rev. Hoffmeister was recorded as cautioning against a "top down" approach where only leadership of the Baptist organizations was serious

---

47. Elwell, *Handbook*, 635.

about unity but their memberships were not. He also suggested that in order for this to be a bottom up approach there needed to be reconciliation drivers in each of the Baptist organizations.[48]

ACHIEVEMENTS

While many challenges face SABA and the unification process, many positive aspects have been realized. For the first time in the history of Baptists in South Africa, different race groups have engaged one another in matters of unification. The regular meetings of SABA gave the different racial groups the opportunity to socialize and share personal concerns as well as to agree to disagree on issues. This would not have been possible with each Baptist organization working independently of the others. The simple activities of sharing meals and traveling together have advanced communication and acceptance.

Many of the misconceptions and suspicions the five organizations had of each other were brought out in the open and cleared. The sharing of ideas and experiences contributed to better understanding. This included sharing of innovative programs, community-based initiatives and international conference participation experiences.

The honesty of the BUSA, as recorded in its statement on April 9, 1999, should be acknowledged. This statement confessed that in the past it has acted wrongfully and sinfully towards Baptist organizations in South Africa. It went as far as admitting a sinful and exclusionary mindset, constitutional inflexibility, and lack of proper communication, as well as deep-seated ignorance.[49]

In evaluating this process, it must be stated that the desired results were not achieved. Despite the good intentions of SABA, the practical manifestations have not been fully realized. While the new dispensation in the country gave impetus to the five Baptist organizations to work towards unification, this is not a good enough reason for reconciliation. Martin Lloyd-Jones,[50] in his commentary *God's Way of Reconciliation*, states that sometimes because of certain circumstances people get together or are driven together, perhaps, by a common need or danger, and they are to be seen talking to one another and cooperating and working

---

48. Baptist Unity, 13.
49. Bulwer Road Minutes, 18–19.
50. Lloyd-Jones, *God's Way*, 279.

together. Perhaps the insecurity of being under a Black administration as well as the fear of being criticized by the international Baptist community for not taking advantage of the conducive political conditions in South Africa in pursing unity are factors that have brought Baptists together.

In the case of SABA, political changes in the country as well as the presence of the BWA in 1998 caused Baptists to begin a process of unification. Once again, should circumstances or biblical motivation determine unification? I think the latter, as Baptists are known to be the "people of the book," people who respect the authority of the Bible.

As noted earlier, the BUSA changed its constitution, hoping that individual churches of the BMSA, ABK, BASA, and BCSA would affiliate directly with it. This was regarded by the other Baptist organizations with suspicion as they felt that the BUSA had little or no regard for the smaller Baptist organizations. One could argue that BUSA was promoting the possibility of a single Baptist organization in South Africa. However, a truly united Baptist organization would have to be negotiated by all the Baptist organizations with a new constitution and a new name. There was some degree of openness by BASA to the goals of SABA. However, BASA was not fully supportive, as it seemed that it wanted to maintain its ethnic identity.

THE WAY FORWARD

If there is to be a united Baptist organization in South Africa, Baptists must first be intentional about unification. They must reflect a commitment to unite with time frames put in place. A time frame will help those who are driving the vision make it a priority. Secondly, negotiators should at all times be transparent and open in matters affecting their understanding of the process as well as the views of their constituencies. Thirdly, Baptists must place God's agenda above everything else. This may seem a highly spiritual recommendation, and indeed it is. As someone who is a minister by vocation and who is deeply committed to the Christian faith, I make this recommendation passionately. As a participant in this process since 1999, I contend that the placing of tradition, history, and the personal interpretation by individuals over the agenda of God poses a serious challenge to the unification of Baptists in South Africa. Fourthly, there must be consensus. Baptists have always applied the principle of consensus in decision-making. The application of this principle leaves much to be desired. Full discussions should and must take place on all levels, including youth meetings, women's meetings and other departmental meetings of the church.

9

Ministry Strategies of the Baptist Association of South Africa

THE INDIAN BAPTIST CHURCH in South Africa is over 100 years old, and the BASA in 2014 will be 100 years old. The church John Rangiah started in 1903 and the many other Indian churches that followed continue to exist as important church communities in the province of Kwa Zulu Natal. The genesis of this ministry was located in a particular spiritual, social, cultural, and political context. Leaders used various strategies that helped this largely ethnic church become what it is today, with its ethnic identity still very much intact.

The new country that Rangiah entered was under the control of the Europeans. The Dutch, who were later called Afrikaners, controlled South Africa through their apartheid policies, and played a major role in shaping the country's religious, political, and cultural landscape. The Afrikaners came to identify themselves with the chosen people of the Old Testament whom God led to the Promised Land.[1] Both Black and White relations were, with minor exceptions, shaped by this brand of Christianity. Consequently the social order in South Africa reflected a system where members of the Dutch Reformed Church understood Christianity as an exclusive and inherited religion that "shored up their group boundaries, nurtured their sense of superiority."[2]

---

1. Regehr, *Perceptions*, 113.
2. Elphick and Davenport, *Christianity*, 2.

For Baptists, The Baptist Union of South Africa, which was a predominantly White-dominated organization, reflected a similar outlook towards Black, Indians, and Colored Baptists. Additionally, the public expression of Christianity for Baptists was with the Baptist Union. Here, too, Black and White Baptist relations were influenced by this monopoly of Christianity. Separate theological institutions were established to cater to the various racial Baptist groups; only the Baptist Union could approve the granting of marriage licenses to non-Baptist Union ministers; and the Baptist Union maintained a very restrictive theological framework that impacted how Blacks, Coloreds, and Indians understood their faith in the socio-political context of South Africa.[3]

Much has been written about the Black-White relations among Baptists prior to the arrival of Rangiah in South Africa. Not much has been written about the entry of Indian Baptists into this socio-political context. Surendra Bhana,[4] in her book *Essays on Indentured Indians in Natal*, provides a number of scholarly essays in the study of Indian indentured labor, the role of labor migration in economic development, and the history of Natal. These essays provide general data on Indians in South Africa. She refers to John Rangiah and the Telugu Baptists who arrived in Natal at the beginning of the nineteenth century but with very little discussion on the mission and its contribution to Christianity in South Africa.[5] Mabel Palmer[6] focuses more on the challenges Indians faced as a people in South Africa. She examines the various laws governing the Indians in Natal and the influence of M. K. Gandhi in South Africa as well as Indian education and culture.

The four categories of influence—spiritual, cultural, social, and political—in the colonized (and later apartheid) South Africa had particular expressions in Natal, where the genesis of the ministry of the BASA was located.

Indian Baptist faith in South Africa, from its inception, was a constant and creative negotiation of an oriental Hindu worldview and a Christian message, communicated mostly through White Baptists and an African context experiencing its own negotiations with European Christianity.

---

3. Hoffmeister and Gurney, *Workshop*, 30.
4. Bhana, *Essays*, 5–224.
5. Ibid., 222.
6. Palmer, *History*, 49–75.

John Rangiah, as well as the Indian indentured laborers, were converts from Hinduism to Christianity, mainly by Americans in India. They were influenced by Americans but lived in a country where distinct cultural and spiritual roots were deeply imbedded in their consciousness. It is with both these western and oriental views of Christianity that they arrived in a largely European and African context. In South Africa and in particular Natal, Baptist Indians found themselves in close proximity to European and African spiritualities.

EUROPEAN SPIRITUALITY

In the sixteenth century the settlers who arrived in South Africa were mainly from the Reformed Church. The history of Christianity in South Africa as recorded by Elphick and Davenport[7] began during this period when Whites first settled at the Cape of Good Hope. They further assert that during this period the Dutch Reformed Church, with minor exceptions, monopolized the public expression of Christianity.

The vast majority of the White colonists understood their salvation as a promise made by God to their ancestors. They felt that Christianity was exclusively a religion for them. This understanding gave them a sense of superiority, which laid the basis for a White-dominated racial order.[8]

In 1895 and 1906 another historical period emerged in South Africa. During this period the British occupied the Cape of Good Hope where South Africa was exposed to an "explosive proliferation of Protestant movements".[9] Newly imported Churches such as the Anglican, Congregational, Baptist, Presbyterian, Methodist, and later the Roman Catholic, Pentecostal, and Lutheran were established in South Africa. The Roman Catholic Church was the first Christian mission to commence work among the indentured Indians, followed by the Methodists and Anglicans. The Lutherans and the Baptists were smaller than the Roman Catholic, Methodist, and Anglican missions.[10] Broadly, the spirituality of the indentured Indians was shaped by their European identity, which was nourished in a European intellectual context. They believed as well that they were superior to the native population and had to civilize them.

---

7. Elphick and Davenport, *Christianity*, 2.
8. Ibid.
9. Ibid., 3.
10. Henning, *Indian*, 154.

AFRICAN SPIRITUALITY

African Christianity according to Elphick and Davenport[11] began during the arrival of White colonists in 1652. Although African Christianity traces its roots to the arrival of Whites, Africans later left the mainline churches' mission organization and developed their own brand of indigenous Christianity. These churches became known as African Initiated Churches (AIC). Bosch[12] is of the opinion that the AICs may be seen as the fifth major Christian church type, after Eastern Orthodox churches, the Roman Catholic Church, the Protestant Reformation churches, and the Pentecostal churches. This group of churches also became known as the African Independent Churches because of their self-reliance, marked by their refusal of foreign financial assistance and leadership. Taylor[13] refers to the son of the founder of the African Presbyterian Church, Mzimba, who commented on the AIC's movement towards an African church by stating that Ethiopianism aimed "to plant a self-supporting, self-governing and self-propagating African church which would produce a truly African type of Christianity suited for the genius and needs of the race, and not a black copy of any European church."

Within the AIC, there are, however, many types of African churches. One such type is the Ethiopian, very similar to the European Protestant church from which it emerged. There are others like the Zion Christian Church (ZCC), which is the largest of the AIC churches.[14] In the Ethiopian type church, infant baptism, reading of liturgies, and the singing of translated European hymns characterize the worship services. Ethiopian type churches are less enthusiastic and emotional in their services than the "prophet healing" African churches.[15]

Other AICs, such as the prophet healing churches or spiritual churches, emphasize the power of the Spirit as healing and prophecy. They are historically connected to the Pentecostal movement, but have, over the years, moved in their own direction, away from Western forms of Pentecostalism.[16]

---

11. Elphick and Davenport, *Christianity*, 2.
12. Bosch, Introduction, 9.
13. Taylor, "Church," 89.
14. Oosthuizen and Hexman, *Religion*, 191.
15. Dyrness and Kärkkäinen, *Dictionary*, 7.
16. Ibid.

The belief in Sangomas, the divine healers of the Zulu people, is also an important facet of Zulu spirituality. It is believed that these sangomas possess supernatural power and can communicate with ancestors on behalf of the people.[17] On the other hand, according to Moodley[18] the amaNazaretha Church (also known as the Shembe Church), now denounces practices such as witchcraft and consultations with Sangomas. However, they still show allegiance to their ancestors. Moodley[19] also makes it clear through his interviews of the members of this church that the community lives in a symbiotic relationship with their ancestors and that the separation between the living and the living-dead is only physical. This means that the living-dead comprise one community and the living consult with the ancestors in all matters that concern them.

The two dominant cultures in South Africa during the early nineteenth century were those of the Africans and Europeans. Indian Baptist missions took place mainly within this European and Zulu cultural context. Natal also has a large English population. Zulus are known for their rich culture and tradition. One of their most distinguishing features is their beadwork, said to be symbolic in that it communicates reprimands, warnings, love, and encouragement.

With the exception of the employer and employee relationship, there was very little meaningful exposure to other cultures. The indentured laborers lived on the Hulett estate and were thus exposed to the culture of the Huletts. The Huletts also mingled with the indentured laborers as they attended the opening of the first Indian Baptist school in Kearsney. Due to this exposure, the Indians adopted a somewhat English way of dressing, although not totally abandoning their traditional dress. Rangiah rode on horseback to the various mission stations. It seems that Indians' contact with the British in India made it easier for them to adopt the English culture.

During the early years of the Indian Baptist ministry, Indians, Coloreds, Blacks, and Whites lived separately. They had their own churches, schools, institutions and racially designated residential areas. Thus there was very little meaningful socializing among the different racial groups. However, the White missionaries such as Judith Morck, Julius

---

17. Moodley, *Shembe, Ancestors, and Christ*, 80–93.
18. Ibid., 93.
19. Ibid.

Forgus, Rev. and Mrs T. D. Pass, and ministers from the Baptist Union worked among the Indian Baptists. The Baptist Union missionary's department, the South African Baptist Missionary Society, appointed Rev. T. D. Pass as its first full-time minister to work in partnership with the Indian Baptist Churches. Pass conducted evangelistic campaigns and trained pastors.

In 2003, the five Baptist organizations formed the South African Baptist Alliance. Since then, the various racial groups have begun interacting in a limited way with one another. However, psychological barriers still exist because of the decades of racial separation, especially on the social level. Although the social and cultural forces in South Africa since the late eighteenth century affected Indian Baptists, the greater force was a political system that impacted every sphere of life.

As discussed earlier, the racial stratification of South African society was an attempt by the government to keep South Africa a White country. The apartheid structure placed Whites at the top of the socio-political ladder, followed by Coloreds, Indians, and then Blacks at the lowest rung.[20] Whites had the privilege of choosing their own government. Coloreds and Indians were offered limited representation in government. In 1980 P. W. Botha, then the State President, established an advisory body called the President's Council where members from Colored, Indian, White and Chinese populations were represented. The right wing members of his National Party objected to this move to share power. They left to start their own party, called the Conservative Party, with the aim of advancing racial policies by fighting for the return of apartheid to its original form. For the right wing politicians, that was a Whites-rule country with all the other racial groups subservient to the White race.

In 1984, P. W. Botha introduced the Tricameral Parliament where Indians and Coloreds were given limited voices in Parliament. A very small percentage of Indians and Coloreds participated in the Tricameral elections. However, the system was put in place and operated between the years 1984 to 1994.[21]

Blacks, through the 1913 Land Act, were also systematically dispossessed of their land and given certain rural areas to live in. Before the Union these were rural areas ruled by local chiefs. They were called

---

20. Moodley, *Shembe, Ancestors, and Christ*, 2.
21. "Tricameral Parliament."

"Native Locations," and Black South Africans were confined to these poor quality areas. Later, under apartheid, these areas were called homelands. Homelands were a creation of the apartheid government, which designated a homeland for every major language in South Africa. There were ten such homelands led by chiefs but controlled by the White government.[22] Natal, the home of the Indian Baptist church, was not a homeland but a quasi-independent Bantustan under the control of its leader, Mangosuthu Gatsha Buthelezi.[23]

Much has been written about the historical, political, cultural and social contexts of South Africa. From a Baptist perspective, Hudson-Reed has written mainly about the Whites and their history of Christianity.[24] Others such as Batts and Chris Parnell, both from the Baptist Union of South Africa, have given sufficient historical information about White Baptist History. Hudson-Reed and most Christian historians on the other hand make only general reference to the history of Black, Colored, and Indian Baptists and their relationship with the dominant White Baptist narrative. Indian Christian history received exposure mainly from Gerald Pillay and G. C. Oosthuizen, who wrote mainly about Pentecostal and general Indian Christian history. Although Pillay makes reference to Indian Baptists, he does not provide an analysis of their contribution to Christianity in South Africa and their impact on the social, cultural and political development.

It is important to examine the specific political context in which Indian Baptists found themselves and how they generated ministry strategies that impacted the four categories described earlier. In order to understand the background of the arrival of Indians to Natal as well as the ministry of the BASA, we must first discuss the specific political context.

The indentured Indian laborers settled largely in the province of Natal. In this province, they were subjected to harsh laws. The general attitude of intolerance of Whites towards the indentured Indians is documented in the writings of Mabel Palmer, C. G. Henning, and Surendra Bhana. When the need for labor was raised in the Natal Colonial government, it was argued that local African labor could be used to meet

---

22. "Homelands."
23. "Mangosuthu Buthelezi."
24. Hudson-Reed, *By Taking Heed*.

this need. Ferguson-Davie[25] refers to a press release in the Natal Mercury dated May 27, 1859 where the Legislative Council discussed the question of labor for the sugar estates. The governor at that time, in a speech, considered the introduction of indentured Indians from the sub-continent to Natal to meet the demand for labor. The response of the Legislative Council to the governor's speech[26] was as follows:

Any Bill introduced to facilitate the introduction of coolies shall receive our warmest support. We must, however, express our disappointment at the absence of any allusion in your Excellency's speech to the want of Native labor, which is pressing so injuriously on the efforts of our agriculturists

The term "coolie," as found in the governor's speech, was used by the colonialists for Indians. A coolie, according to the compact Oxford Dictionary, is a Hindi word meaning day laborer and more specifically an unskilled native laborer in India, China, and some other Asian countries. It can also mean a person from the Indian subcontinent or of Indian descent. In the South African context, the word "coolie" is today viewed as a racial slur on Indians.

Despite the strong case put forward by many in the Natal Colonial Government to settle for local African labor, the decision to allow Indians into South Africa to meet the labor crisis won the day. In 1859 there were three laws passed that dealt with the Indian labor immigration. Law 13 dealt with the introduction of immigrants from territories east of the Cape of Good Hope; Law 14 dealt with the introduction of laborers from India; and Law 15 dealt with enabling persons to introduce, at their own expense, immigrants from India.[27] This paved the way for the arrival of indentured laborers. The first group of indentured Indians arrived in 1860.

From the outset in Natal, Whites saw Indians as "the other," as an alien group of people. Sixty-five years later, comments by politicians such as D. F. Malan, the Minister of the Interior in 1925, reflected a negative attitude towards the Indians in South Africa. He remarked, "The Indian, as a race in this country, is an alien element in the population."[28] Violet Wetherell is quoted by Dhupelia-Meshrie as stating:

---

25. Ferguson-Davie, *History*, 10.
26. Ibid.
27. Ibid., 11.
28. Dhupelia-Mesthrie, *From Fields to Freedom*, 13.

> The Indian has always been a separate element in South African life ... The Indian has remained apart, racially, linguistically, religiously. He has kept his blood pure and intermarried neither with Native nor European; though he speaks English, he has adhered to his own religions ... His ancient beliefs are wide gulf between the Indian and the European. A Mohammedanism [sic] permit of polygamy which is abhorrent to western standards ... Hinduism involves the worship of the cow, a conception which is alien to the European.[29]

Malan is partly correct in his assertion that Indians have always been a separate element in South Africa. However, the reality was also that the attitudes of Whites towards them were not welcoming, and the many laws of the Natal government made it difficult for Indians to interact with Whites. It was difficult for the Indians under such conditions to become a full part of the South African community.

Anti-Indian attitudes and anti-Indian legislation increased. Members of the Natal Colonial Government objected to the continuation of the indentured labor system. One of the most prominent politicians in the Natal Colony, Mr. Harry Escombe, became one of the strongest opponents of Indian immigration to the Natal Colony. In Escombe's[30] earlier speech in 1884 he remarked on the contribution Indians had made on an area of land that the indentured laborers worked on: "They have turned a sandy delta into a useful, profitable, productive piece of land and have become a useful and exemplary section of the community." Escombe[31] later changed his position on the immigration issue and said, "This country (Natal) was meant for Europeans and was never intended to be an Asiatic Colony." But when Escombe became the prime minister of Natal he changed his position again, stating, "With regards to the time-expired Indians, I do not think it ought to be compulsory for any man to go to any part of the world, save for a crime for which he can be transported."[32]

On the matter of extending the contract for indentured Indians, Mr. Robert Topham of Pietermaritzburg objected to the extension of the indentured labor system, stating:

> If the importation of Indians cannot be suppressed, laborers would be a great point gained. This was intended from the first, but on account

---

29. Ibid., 15.
30. Henning, *Indian*, 94.
31. Ibid.
32. Ferguson-Davie, *History*, 23.

of the laxity of those through whom the coolie labor was passing . . . this intention was allowed to slide.[33]

Topham was of the opinion that local Africans should have been employed from the start. Others, such as Mr. F. A. Hathorn, chairman of the Pietermaritzburg Chamber of Commerce in Natal, supported the views of Topham, which reflected anti-Indian sentiments. Hathorn said, "I would make the return of the Indian compulsory after ten years."[34] There were also others who provided evidence to the Wragg Commission. In 1885 the Wragg Commission was appointed by the colonial government to deal with some of the grievances of the indentured laborers. There were some Whites who wanted to represent the Indians in a negative light to the Commission. The evidence Whites cited included that Indians were unsanitary; that they sold liquor to natives and were themselves given to drink; that they were dishonest; and that they undercut European shopkeepers.[35]

The Wragg Commission could not find any evidence that Indians sold more liquor to the Africans than any other people, and those who had special knowledge of the Indians could not agree with the accusation that Indians were dishonest.

There were, however, those in the Natal Colonial Government who supported legislation that encouraged the indentured labor system and argued against the return of the laborers to India after their contracts expired. Mr. Henry Binns, chairman of the Indian Immigration Trust Board (afterwards Prime Minister of Natal); Mr. C. T. Saner, chairman of the Victoria Planters' Association; Hon. M. H. Gallway, Attorney-General (member of the Coolie Commission of 1872); and Mr. J. R. Saunders, one of the Commissioners who had been a member of the Legislative Council when the Indian immigrants first arrived, were important officials in the Natal Colonial Government who represented a positive voice for the Indentured Indians.

Despite the rigorous debates in the Natal Colonial Government about the Indentured Labor System, Indians were offered the option after five years to be free from their contractual agreement with their employers or they could sign another five-year agreement. Thereafter they could become citizens of the colony. Although there were a number of indentured

---

33. Ibid., 22.
34. Ibid., 23.
35. Ibid., 24.

Indians who returned to India after their contracts expired, the majority of the Indians who were Baptists on Sir James Liege Hulett's tea estate remained as employees of the Huletts. Rangiah wrote that at the end of their contracts, the majority "re-indentured" themselves while a few reurned to India.[36] Although there were many incidents of ill-treatment by the colonial employers throughout Natal, which resulted in the return of thousands of indentured Indians to India, there were also those who decided to remain in South Africa. However, those who remained were subject to laws that impeded their movement and growth.

Immigrant Indians in South Africa were divided socially. The vast majority were indentured laborers. A second group, the business class, did not have any social relations with the indentured laborers. These merchants resisted the generalized impartial attitudes of Whites towards them. They went to the extent of calling themselves "Arabs" and wore flowing robes. A third group was comprised of merchants and Parsi clerks. They called themselves "Persians." These latter two groups wanted to be distinguished from the indentured laborers.[37]

GANDHI IN SOUTH AFRICA

Mohandas K. Gandhi came to South Africa in 1893 as a barrister to help with a civil suit in Pretoria. His clients were a group of Indian merchants facing discriminatory legislation. After settling the law case that he'd come to work on, Gandhi prepared to leave for India. However, he was persuaded to stay longer as the bill, which sought to deprive Indians of their right to elect members of the Assembly, was under threat.[38]

When traveling by train from Durban to Pretoria, Gandhi was manhandled off the train by a policeman.[39] When he boarded another train with the assistance of Indian friends, he was relegated to an inferior seat and was violently assaulted by the conductor because of his refusal to change seats again. Some White passengers intervened, saving him from further violent attacks.[40]

36. Rangiah, *Reports*, 5.
37. Polak et al., *Gandhi*, 27.
38. Ibid.
39. Ibid., 28.
40. Ibid., 25.

His experience in South Africa did not deter him from championing the cause of Indians in South Africa. When the Colonial government began tightening its grip on Indians, Gandhi, together with the organization Natal Indian Congress, engaged in protests. Their resistance was termed "satyagraha," which meant "the force which is born of Truth and Love or non-violence."[41]

Polak, Brailsfor, and Lawrence[42] recorded that among the volunteers who were enrolled to oppose this Bill were Natal-born Indians who were mostly Christians. Previously these Christians were excluded from public activity "because of their lowly origin." It seemed that the indentured Indians not only suffered discrimination under the Natal Colonial government, but were also treated as separate from their fellow Indians (mainly merchants and clerks), because of their economic and educational status.

While this was the case on a national level, indentured laborers in the Baptist Association of South Africa had a different experience at Kearsney with their landlord. Sir James Liege Hulett, Rangiah's landlord, favored the indentured labor system. He took good care of these poor and poorly educated Indians, in stark contrast to the treatment Indians received from their fellow Indians in the surrounding estates. Indians in Durban lived in accommodations that were unsatisfactory. In 1864 the municipality erected "barracks" for their Indian laborers, described by Henning[43] as primitive and a "permanent blemish on Western values."

There is no record of ill treatment by the Huletts of the Indians. Rangiah described Hulett as a "liberal minded and benevolent gentleman." It is also recorded that Hulett kept between twelve and fifteen Indian children in his house where he and his wife took care of them.[44] On the other hand, Dhupelia-Mesthrie[45] reports that women laborers on the tea estate received half the wages men were given and that during the picking season, women worked for about eleven to thirteen hours a day. Nevertheless the indentured laborers on Hulett's estate found a home in Natal and went on to contribute to the economic, spiritual, cultural,

---

41. Dhupelia-Mesthrie, *From Fields to Freedom*, 21.
42. Polak et al., *Gandhi*.
43. Henning, *Indian*, 5.
44. Rangiah, *NIBA News*, 14.
45. Dhupelia-Mesthrie, *From Fields to Freedom*, 9.

132 VISION IN PROGRESS

and social development of the Natal North Coast region. From a political perspective, the fate of these Indians was in the hands of the colonial government. The general attitude of the colonial government and the business sector was not very welcoming towards the Indians. Sir James Liege Hulett, it seemed, was more accommodating.

STRATEGIES OF LEADERS

The NIBA News[46] provides a comprehensive record of John Rangiah's ministry among the indentured Indians in Natal. It portrays a man with a deep commitment to advancing the spiritual development of the indentured laborers beginning from the time he accepted the offer to go to Natal as a missionary in 1903 until his death in 1915. In India, he made thorough preparation for the trip to Natal. He took many speaking engagements at various churches in Ramapatnam, Ongole, Bapatla, Venukonda, Narsaraopet, Cumbum and Kutnool. His home church, Lone Star Baptist Church in Nellore, was particularly happy that one of its own members was being sent as a foreign missionary to South Africa.[47]

Before his departure, Rangiah wrote to Mr. W. Spencer Walton, the superintendent of the South African General Mission, informing him of his intention to serve as a missionary in Natal.[48] In 1903, when Rangiah, his wife, Kanakamma, and two children arrived in Durban on the ship *Safari*, he was overwhelmed by the task. Not knowing about their future in a foreign country, Rangiah expressed what he felt and thought prior to disembarking:

> Where shall I go? Who will receive us in this vast and strange Land? Did Mr. Walton receive my letter? Even so will he receive me gladly? O Thou my Master of the Gospel, who is worthy of this great work? I cannot bear the weight of this great call. The Telugu Baptist Churches in India, which have sent me to propagate the Gospel, have they enough strength to carry on this great work? Thou O Lord, Thou alone, Thy Spirit alone, can bring salvation to many souls here and glory to thy name. Sanctify me, O Lord and in Thy graciousness use Thy servant for Thy sake.[49]

46. Rangiah, *NIBA News*, 2–15.
47. Ibid., 9.
48. Ibid., 8.
49. Ibid., 11.

Dayadharum[50] refers to Donald McGavran's homogenous unit theory, introduced much later than Rangiah's time, which advocated homogenous church planting. A homogeneous unit often means a group that shares a common language, culture, or other characteristic that diferentiates it from other groups.[51] The major characteristic of indentured Baptists was that they spoke mainly Telugu. Given the already stratified South African society, was this theory helpful? And how did it affect race relations? From 1903 to 1915, Rangiah established eight homogenous churches. Below are the statistics of these churches:[52]

Church	Date Established	Pastor	Membership
Kearsney	12/27/1903	J. Rangiah	64
Verulam	05/22/1904	K. Daniel	32
Darnall	06/12/1904	A. Reuben	30
Durban	10/30/1904	Yellamanda	15
Stanger	12/25/1904		12
Tinley Manor	05/10/1908	K. David	12
Dundee	06/05/1908	T. C. Tyler	21
Amatikuli	01/11/1909	P. Reddy	12

These churches were established in areas where there were mainly Indians living. The pastors were Indians who spoke the Telugu language. Although this represents a significant growth in the number of churches established by Rangiah within a period of twelve years, the homogenous unit principle he employed did little to encourage race relations among the races, especially the indigenous African people. This principle did aid in the the spiritual development of a particular linguistic, ethnic group and denomination, the Telugu Indian Baptist. It seems this was a case of applying a sociological observation as a starting point for developing a church planting strategy. The question is, Where is the voice of Scripture in this? There are some who challenge the homogenous unit theory, arguing that it replaces biblical theology with principles derived from sociology and advocates techniques that come close to subverting the most fundamental principles of the gospel.[53]

50. Dayadharum, "Role," 150.
51. McGavran, *Understanding Church Growth*, 5.
52. Rangiah, *NIBA News*, 19–27.
53. Dayadharum, "Role," 150.

Greg Goss[54] argues:

> The problem with this approach is that homogeneous evangelism creates an homogeneous church, and many would see such a church as a distortion of the gospel where there is no such thing as Jew or Greek, rich or poor, slave or free. Homogeneity increases inclusion, but it also increases exclusion. While people are more likely to become Christians without dealing with cultural differences, they are more likely to grow spiritually as they deal with and learn from these differences.

Currently the BASA has a membership of largely ethnic Indians who are content to be with their own kind with regard to worship. Although in 2001, Baptists in South Africa formed the South African Baptist Alliance where the five Baptist organizations decided to cooperate, they (with the exception of a few churches) have maintained their racial, ethnic, and linguistic identities. The evangelism used by Rangiah and the churches he established has not only produced a homogenous unit church in South Africa but has created a particular understanding of the gospel that is similar to the Baptist Union's earlier approach to homogenous unit church planting.

Dayadharum[55] maintains that McGavran's homogenous unit principle as applied by John Rangiah and his son Theophilius contributed to the growth and development of the Indian Baptist Church in South Africa, though it does appear that such a principle promotes a kind of spiritual "apartheid" in the churches. Dayadharum argues that McGavaran, who was a missionary in India, was very aware of the caste system in Indian culture and that he arrived at the conclusion that this was the most effective principle for church planting in India.

Although quantitatively the church grew significantly in India using the homogenous unit principle under the caste system (and the same was true of the Indian Baptist Church in South Africa under the Rangiahs), this principle had two weaknesses. First, it had no biblical basis, and second, it did not prepare the church for the social, cultural, and political changes that would eventually take place in South Africa. The two Indian Baptist organizations in South Africa, BASA and BMSA, are still largely

---

54. Goss, "Principles."
55. Dayadharum, "Role," 153.

ethnically Indian. Any suggestion to embrace other cultures and races is generally not accommodated with great enthusiasm.

LANGUAGE

At the beginning of the nineteenth century in South Africa there were many African languages. The main languages spoken in Natal during this period were English, Afrikaans, and Zulu. When the Indians arrived at the end of the nineteenth and early twentieth century to Natal, the following eastern languages were mainly spoken: Hindi, Arabic, Gujarati, Sanskrit, Tamil, Telugu and Urdu. Seventy-one percent of the Indians who embarked from Madras spoke Tamil; 25 percent spoke Telugu.[56] The indentured Baptist Indians, who were mainly from the south of India, spoke Telugu with a few speaking Tamil. The Indian Baptists at Kearsney experienced a language barrier when their landlord, Sir J. L. Hulett, attempted to provide white Wesleyan ministers who spoke only English to minister to the Telugus.[57]

Dayadharum[58] wrote that Rangiah used the Telugu language that was spoken by the indentured Indians to enhance his work in South Africa. Dayadharum, on the issue of language, argued against using Donald McGavran's theory that churches tend to develop more rapidly when people speak the same language and come from the same culture. Dayadharum[59] further describes the Telugu language, using the words of Bishop Azariah, a Tamilian educator: "The Telugu language, which is liquid and melodious, has sometimes been called the Italian of the East and their culture is rich in poetry, music and fine literature." Rangiah not only spoke and preached in Telugu, but, as noted earlier, he wrote lyrics in the Telugu language. The early development of the Indian Baptist Church in South Africa in its application of McGravan's theory of church growth, as argued by Dayadharum, proved to be true.

Rangiah held religious meetings in the various parts of Natal. He called these meetings Festivals. He believed that "the Telugu mind in general is simple and inclined to cheerfulness and the hard-working laborers especially need joyous diversion. So our Christian Festivals help us

56. Bhana, *Essays*, 192.
57. Rangiah, *NIBA News*, 8.
58. Dayadharum, "Role," 55.
59. Ibid., 56.

greatly in refreshing both mind and spirit."[60] These festivals were held at Christmas, New Year's Day, and Easter. Another festival, called "Gospel Festival," was held annually in October.

In addition to the regular services at the various churches, Rangiah introduced services on weekdays. Called "cottage meetings," they were held in the homes of members. Prior to Rangiah's arrival to Kearnsey, he, together with a White minister, Rev. Tomlinson, conducted prayer and evangelistic services in the various suburbs of Durban. Rangiah also sought and received permission from the Protector of Indian Immigrants, Mr. J. Polkinghorn, to conduct evangelistic meetings with Indian immigrants in the ships and at the immigration depot.

Theophilius Rangiah's ministry among the indentured laborers was challenging, as these laborers "were poor, majority illiterate (did not even know how to read Telugu), and unrefined in many ways."[61] Through the influence of his mother, Theophilius adapted to the educational level of his congregants and began his ministry in Natal. As an itinerant, Theophilius traveled on horseback to the various regions in Natal.

Theophilius emphasized the importance of organization. He assisted in re-organizing several churches in the BASA. Timothy[62] records that Theophilius re-organized four churches: Hillary, Kearnsey, Umhlali, and the Durban work. His work among the churches was also well planned. Since many of the churches that his father established were located on estates owned by Whites, Theophilius "approached the European masters and managers of these various estates" and encouraged them to get involved in the spiritual welfare of their Christian laborers.[63] Three preachers—B. Philip, M. Zachariah and Joshua—were assigned to preach and to conduct cottage meetings, prayer meetings, and other religious services among the laborers, thus minimizing the workload for Theophilius. He supervised the work of these pastors as well as other lay leaders who were serving in the churches established by his father.

The strategy Theophilius employed focused on identifying capable men, nurturing and training them, and then appointing them as pastors. Although no women were appointed to lead churches, Theophilius's

---

60. Rangiah, *NIBA News*, 15.
61. Ibid., 36.
62. Timothy, *Risecliff*, 6.
63. Rangiah, *NIBA News*, 37.

mother, Kanakamma played a leading role in the mission work, which included visiting churches and providing spiritual support for the leaders. Theophilius also visited the churches his father had established and continued building on his father's foundation. He also established a relationship with the White Baptist Union, and during his tenure the Natal Indian Baptist Association became an affiliate member of the Baptist Union of South Africa.[64]

Theophilius Rangiah established three churches: Glendale Baptist Church (1922), Umhlali Baptist Church (1923), and the Baptist Church in North Street, Durban (1940).[65] Two of the churches, Glendale Baptist and the church in North Street, Durban had a combined membership of 360. The Umhlali Baptist Church is described as small.[66] Theophilius also applied the homogenous unit principle in the establishment of the above-named churches. Dayadharum[67] in an interview with Theophilius' son-in-law, N. M. Israel, quotes Israel as describing Theophilius as follows:

> He was bold and always composed. Not even physical danger unmanned him. Haphazard work, ill-prepared messages, shabby dress, unpunctuality, ambiguity, and slovenly expression were not tolerated by him. He was meticulous to the smallest detail. His dress, bearing and speech were always dignified. He was a gifted organizer. He regarded the executive as the highest authority in the Association. Rarely did he enter the debate in the executive. He was at home with the rich and the poor alike.

Israel's description of Theophilius Rangiah as an organizer is evident in Rangiah's approach to ministry. He is also described by his son Mimosthram[68] and by Timothy[69] as a very organized person.

When Theophilius returned to India in 1927 to complete his degree, he changed his major from law and completed a Bachelor of Arts degree with the inclusion of theology courses.[70] He served as the manager of the Kearsney Indian School that was established by his father. His brother, T.

---

64. Ibid.
65. Rangiah, *NIBA News*, 38–42.
66. Ibid., 41.
67. Dayadharum, "Role," 94.
68. Rangiah, *NIBA News*, 37.
69. Timothy, *Silver Jubilee*, 4–5.
70. Rangiah, *NIBA News*, 43.

R. Rangiah, served as the principal of this school. The school in Kearsney was divided into three classes. The first class was assigned for young children, the second for older children, and the third for youth. Because of lack of space, classes were held under the trees.[71] Theophilius devoted much of his time trying to resolve the conflict between the Natal Indian Baptist Association and the Indian Baptist Mission, but was unsuccessful.

DAVID NEWTON NATHANIEL

Like his predecessor, David Nathaniel visited all the churches that were established by the Rangiahs. He provided pastoral care for the many who were discouraged by the death of Theophilus Rangiah. Many of the indentured laborers had backslidden; through the pastoral visits of Nathaniel, many returned to the church. The NIBA News[72] describes Nathaniel as follows: "His quiet talks, winsome nature, touching sermons and above all his humility has brought many backsliders to the fold." Nathaniel carried out the many pastoral responsibilities that were carried out by the Rangiahs, such as conducting prayer and thanksgiving services and cottage meetings. He also conducted weddings, baptized members, and held Bible studies.

One significant strategy that Nathaniel employed was to provide theological education for the Indian Baptists. He arrived in Natal having completed a Bachelor of Divinity degree, and later he completed the Master of Divinity degree at the University of Durban-Westville. It is recorded[73] that on July 18–20, 1952, he held Bible classes that included a series of three lectures on the book of Ruth. On August 30–31, 1952, he gave two lectures in St. Aidens Hall in Durban as well as at the Baptist Church in North Street Durban. His lecture included a study on "Christ and Karl Marx" and "Christ Amidst Chaos." Four months later, on December 15–17, he presented another lecture focusing on the book of Esther. At the Kearsney Baptist Church his lectures on the gospel of Matthew drew audiences from the White clergy and intellectual community.

Nathaniel wrote a significant book, *For The Preacher in the Making*, with the poor and the not-so-educated Indian Christians in mind. Nathaniel believed that it was important to provide these Christians with

---

71. Dayadharum, "Role," 101.
72. Rangiah, *NIBA News*, 50.
73. Ibid.

resources for preaching. His book provided helpful suggestions and sermon outlines and sample sermons, as well as information on how to use stories in a sermon.[74]

Nathaniel started the newsletter *The NIBA News*, which had a devotional article as well as reports on the churches and departments of the association. It included a financial report of the Sunday School Department of the association. Nathaniel wrote the devotional articles on Christmas, Easter, and New Year's. They were by and large inspiring and always grounded in Scripture, which reflected his sound theological training.

From 1951 to 1953, Nathaniel's work among the Indian Baptists produced a renewed interest in the church. During this period, 112 people embraced the Christian faith, and eight churches recorded increases in membership, renewal and consecration of lives, and a renewed interest in Bible classes. At Kearsney, new hymns, composed by Nathaniel, were used in worship services. In the Glendale Church it was recorded that there were 260 adults and 100 children. During this period there were also 31 who were baptized. The elders at this church had a renewed sense of excitement. They visited various homes, especially in the Trans-Umvoti district of Natal. The membership at the Darnall Baptist Church was 144 adults and forty-nine children. The church at Tinley Manor recorded a membership of 100 adults with fifteen children; at Umhlali, seventy-five adults, fifteen children; at Durban, 265 adults, seventy children; and at Dannhauser, twenty-nine adults, thirty children.[75]

During Nathaniel's ministry, the BASA grew significantly. Timothy[76] refers to the BUSA's T. D. Pass's statement about the growth of BASA under Nathaniel's leadership. He stated, "Under his inspired leadership, linked with unflagging labor and assisted by consecrated laymen and, later, by the influx of several fully trained ministers, the Association has shown unprecedented growth." During Nathaniel's time, the following joined BASA: Reverends R. Ellaya, R. Jayakaram, Manuel Jacob, Reuben Steven, H. Pretorius, D. Jeevarathnam, C. Joseph, D. James, and T. Rhandram. During this period, Rev. Dixon James was a regular speaker on a Christian radio program called "Checkpoint." The clergy mentioned above all assisted in the growth and expansion of the work of BASA. Between 1953

---

74. Nathaniel, *For the Preacher in the Making*, 1–66.
75. Ibid., 48–50.
76. Timothy, *Risecliff*, 8.

and 1975, BASA membership increased by 400 percent, from 610 to 1700 baptized members.[77]

There is no record of any of the Indian-born missionaries questioning or challenging South Africa's unjust and discriminatory laws.

MIMOSTHRAM RANGIAH

Mimosthram Rangiah, the grandson of John Rangiah, served BASA for almost fifty years, most significantly as its president for about twenty years. As a former school teacher and school principal, Rangiah was a member of the Tongaat Baptist Church and later became its pastor. He was responsible for the building of a beautiful building for the Tongaat Baptist Church. In 1953 Rangiah was tasked with writing the history of the Natal Indian Baptist Association for its Golden Jubilee brochure. Much of the information in this book is derived from that brochure.

One of the significant contributions Rangiah made to the Indian Baptist Church was vernacular music. Like his father, Theophilius, Mimosthram composed and arranged the music of several Telugu songs. At the annual Easter eisteddfod all the BASA churches met for the Easter service and later in the day the churches would present songs in a singing competition. Rangiah's choir and musical band almost always placed first. In 1978 Rangiah and his choir presented vernacular songs on the Indian radio station Radio Lotus.

NOAH MOSES ISRAEL

Noah Moses Israel is the great-son-in-law of John Rangiah. He married Rajithamma Rangiah. Israel, an ex-school teacher, is an important lay person in the history of the Indian Baptist Church in South Africa. He served the BASA in various capacities for almost fifty years, leading it from 2003 to 2005. Under his presidency, the BASA celebrated its centenary. Israel took some theological courses at the Durban Bible College. He was among the first batch of students who attended evening classes at this College.

In 1994, when South Africa held its first democratic elections, Israel initiated talks between BASA and BMSA with the hope of achieving closer cooperation between the two Indian Baptist organizations. Israel

---

77. Ibid., 9.

in 2003 played the role of John Rangiah in a radio play titled *Behold the Indian Baptist*. It aired on East Coast Radio and Radio Highveld. It also aired on radio stations in India and Pakistan.[78] In 2004, at the Baptist World Alliance's Heritage Commission in Seoul, South Korea, Israel presented the paper "John Rangiah and a Century of Indian Baptist Work in Africa." He also served on the BWA's Heritage Commission.[79]

Noah Israel is considered by many as the historian of the Indian Baptist Church. He has written numerous articles on the history of the BASA, many of which appear in micro-narratives and church brochures. In 2003, he addressed the Heritage Commission of the BWA on the history of the Indian Baptists in South Africa. In addition to his contribution to the preservation of Indian Baptist history, Israel has represented the BASA on numerous occasions at Baptist Union executive meetings. He has championed the Indian Baptist heritage as well as its historical significance both at these executive meetings and among the Indian Baptist churches generally. He has served BASA in various capacities, including as vice-president, president, General Secretary, and as the editor of various BASA brochures.

ANTHONY POLIAH

Anthony Poliah served as president of the BASA from 1996 to 2000. Prior to his role as president, he served as a leader of Jehovah Nilayam Baptist Church in Glendale, was principal of the BASA Bible College, served as associate pastor of Stanger Manor Baptist Church in Stanger, and held various other positions in the BASA.

He represented the BASA at the SABA meetings in 1998 and in the same year was the program director of the Baptist World Alliance rally in Durban. He also inducted the first woman, Evelyn Maistry, into the ministry of the BASA.

Poliah's administrative and organizational skills contributed to the ministry of the BASA. As a chairperson at the BASA executive committee meetings, he minimized the length of these meetings by 50 percent, coordinated the BASA Bible College program, and organized seminars and

78. Israel, letter to author, 2008.
79. Ibid.

the BASA Bible College graduation. He also promoted closer cooperation with the BMSA.[80]

RODNEY RAGWAN

I was born in 1965 in Stanger, Natal. The great-grandson of David Rajanna, an Indian indentured laborer, I was trained as a minister and served Marriannhill Baptist Church (now called Parousia Baptist Church) for fourteen and a half years. I served the BASA in various capacities, becoming its president in 2001. During my tenure, I sought membership in international organizations. In 2001 I traveled to Washington, DC in the USA to engage in discussions with the BWA about membership. At the General Council of the BWA, held in Spain in 2001, BASA was formally accepted into BWA membership. I also applied on behalf of BASA for membership in the All Africa Baptist Fellowship, a regional body of the BWA. In 2001, this was granted. I was elected to serve on various committees of the BWA, such as the General Council, 21st Century Think Tank Committee, and the Development Committee.[81]

I facilitated two visits of BASA leaders to the USA. The first was a visit to North Carolina where BASA pastors had the opportunity to preach and participate in a Pastors' Conference.[82] The second was undertaken by the BASA cabinet. It included Noah Moses Israel, Rajie Israel, Richard Nathaniel, Marge Nathaniel, Harold T. Paul, and Richard Amos. This visit included the signing of a partnership agreement between the BASA and International Ministries, the mission agency of the American Baptist Churches, USA. During this visit, BASA and the BMSA met in Los Angeles, where Dr. Samuel Chetti, executive minister of the Los Angeles Baptist Association, sponsored a meeting of BASA and BMSA. Rev. Desmond Hoffmeister, the former General Secretary of the Baptist Convention of South Africa, facilitated the discussion, the purpose of which was to facilitate unity between the two organizations, which split in 1914.[83]

As part of my strategy, I advocated the theological training of leaders in the BASA. I secured resources for theological education for the

---

80. Israel, letter.
81. Ragwan, *In His Service*, 50–53.
82. Ibid., 51.
83. Ibid., 64–66.

BASA leaders, and in 2001, four leaders were enrolled at Universities in South Africa.[84]

ASSESSING THE MINISTRY STRATEGY OF BASA

Did the ministry strategies of these various leaders impact South Africa? Two key factors that will assist in responding to this question are ethnocentricity and theological orientation. Ethnocentricity[85] is defined as (1) "the belief in the inherent superiority of one's own ethnic group or culture" (2) "a tendency to view alien groups or cultures from the perspective of one's own." It does not seem that the leaders in any way believed in the superiority of their ethnicity. Rather it seems that they viewed the other groups such as the Blacks, Coloreds, and Whites from an Indian perspective and from within the socio-political reality of South Africa at that time.

John Rangiah, Theophilius Rangiah, and David Newton Nathaniel, as well as each of the other significant leaders who followed, used a strategy that seemed to have led to an ethnocentric organization. Over the years, with the exception of a few churches and leaders who ministered to Blacks, BASA existed as a church for Indians. However, there are indications that it is currently moving towards being more inclusive of other races, especially Blacks. It has been more open to other sub-cultures or other language groups that speak Tamil, Hindi, and Guajarati.[86]

From the inception of the Indian Baptist church in South Africa in 1903, and more specifically of the BASA under John Rangiah, Indian leaders were identified, trained, and appointed to Indian Churches. It does seem that during Rangiah's work in Natal, the Babatha Rebellion in the early twentieth century put a sense of fear in the Indian indentured Baptists. The NIBA News[87] states that during the rebellion, Mrs. Rangiah and her children had to spend the night in the bush because of their fear of the Zulus. The Babatha Rebellion probably caused Rangiah and his successors some fear, thus they concentrated their efforts on providing spiritual care for Indians. The BASA history does not show any record of

---

84. Ibid., 49.
85. Dictionary.com.
86. Dayadharum, "Role," 128.
87. Rangiah, *NIBA News*, 17.

Rangiah or the two missionaries who followed him serving the spiritual needs of Blacks.

According to Timothy,[88] seven of the eight pastors during Nathaniel's ministry serving the BASA churches were Indians; the other was a so-called Colored. A second possible reason for the ethnocentric strategy is the language barrier. Although the three Indian-born missionaries spoke English, the indentured laborers spoke mainly Telugu, so including Zulus in Indian Churches would have been challenging for both Indians and Blacks. However, over the years, many Indian Baptists learned to speak the Zulu language, though no attempts as of 2006 were made by BASA to open its mission to the Zulus in Natal, although individual churches within the BASA have become more inclusive in their membership.

With regard to Rangiah's method of church planting within the Indian indentured laborer community, it yielded results, as reported in the NIBA News.[89] Here too, his was an ethnocentric approach, one that can be compared to McGavaran's previously cited homogenous principle. Rangiah's use of the Telugu language, music, drama, festivals, and cottage meetings, as well as an emphasis on Bible study, contributed to the growth of the churches that shared all the elements in McGavaran's church planting principles.

The strategy employed by almost all BASA leaders contributed to Christianity in South Africa. During John Rangiah's work, the membership, according to NIBA News,[90] stood at 208, but it plateaued after the death of John Rangiah. The arrival of his son, Theophilius Rangiah, saw the BASA increase from 208 to 610 members. The greatest growth came during Nathaniel's ministry. From 1953 to 1975, BASA's membership grew from 610 to 1700. This figure included only baptized members, excluding children, which numbered 1000.[91]

Timothy states[92] that when Theophilius Rangiah died, BASA was without a clergy, and it was during this transitional period that the BASA was experiencing the loss of members. Laymen assumed the leadership of the organization, but this did not prevent members from leaving for

---

88. Timothy, *Risecliff*, 9.
89. Rangiah, *NIBA News*, 19–27.
90. Ibid.
91. Timothy, *Risecliff*, 8.
92. Ibid.

other denominations. Timothy[93] refers to Oosthuizen's statement about this: "When Baptist membership was at its lowest in 1946, Pentecostalism was making one of its most spectacular increases." It took Rev. Nathaniel, a theologically trained clergyperson, to consolidate the work of BASA and build it to where it had a 400 percent increase in its membership since Theophilius Rangiah's leadership.[94]

Beyond what it has contributed to the church in South Africa, BASA has contributed to South African culture. The medium of communicating the gospel in the vernacular language and the use of drama and festivals has increased awareness among the South African population of this culture. On a national level, in 1972, the grandson of John Rangiah, Mimosthram Rangiah, was invited to broadcast a special Easter program on national radio and then a Christmas program in 1975 and 1977. These broadcasts included songs in Telugu, accompanied by Rangiah's band. In 1976 Rev. Dixon James, a BASA clergyperson, was a regular preacher on Transworld Radio.[95] In 1992, I myself presented three devotional sermons on a national television program called "Epilogue."

As mentioned earlier, Noah Moses Israel and Mimosthram Rangiah were involved in the writing of BASA history, which appears in the NIBA News and Diamond and Golden Jubilee brochures. They provided recordings of the events and contributions of the leaders to the BASA work, and these are good for posterity. However, they were written from the perspective of the dominant members and thus have the propensity to affirm the ethnocentric nature of the work of the BASA. Additionally, these histories lack historical and theological analysis.

Maintaining the ethnocentricity of the organization adversely affected it, as leaders engaged in dialogue only among themselves. No new voices from outside of BASA were being heard, which prevented exposure to new perspectives on critical issues. Perspectives from younger leaders were received cautiously. As noted, I, upon being elected president in 2001, sought membership in BWA, All Africa Baptist Fellowship, and the American Baptist Churches, USA and its mission agency. I also established a relationship with the Los Angeles Baptist Association and the Cabarrus Baptist Association. The linking of BASA to all these

---

93. Ibid., 4.
94. Ibid., 8.
95. Ibid., 11.

international organizations assisted in broadening the world view of the BASA. Leaders are now attending meetings and conferences overseas. The fruits of these partnerships are being experienced. But although the BASA is being exposed to the international community, it has still not moved significantly beyond its ethnocentricity.

BASA contributed significantly to the spiritual and cultural (as well as the economic) development of Christianity among Indians, but that is where it appears to stop. Unfortunately the three Indian-born missionaries did not respond to the socio-political issues in South Africa. The ethnocentric approach to mission work in South Africa was shaped by a particular theology that the Indian-born missionaries carried with them from India. The South African-born Indian leaders were very much influenced by the conservative evangelical theology advanced by the BUSA.

THEOLOGICAL ORIENTATION

From the beginning of the Baptist movement in the seventeenth century, the articles of faith that guided the American Baptist Churches were as follows: (1) *The living Christ is the final judge of a person's belief and actions;* (2) *The Bible is a dynamic, not a static, document that needs to be interpreted for every age;* (3) *The separation of church and state is good both for the church and the state, and it promotes the common good of all citizens;* (4) *Non-conformity to majority opinion is part of the Baptist heritage, and to submit Baptist theology to majority vote is to betray the heritage of people called Baptists;* and (5) *The local church is free to make its own decisions under the Lordship of Christ; theological diversity among Baptists is a strength.*[96]

John Rangiah's theology was guided to a large extent by the above articles of faith and in particular by article 3, which states that *the separation of church and state is good both for the church and the state and promotes the common good of all citizens.* Given the agenda of the South African government to keep South Africa white, BASA and its leaders have perhaps understood this article of faith to mean that the church should not challenge the state on laws that discriminated against them. In any case, neither BASA nor its leaders made any significant protest against the state for its discriminatory laws against Indians, Blacks, and Coloreds. On the other hand, it was probably challenging for the three Indian-born missionaries

---

96. Coalition for Baptist Principles, "Declaration."

to protest against the injustices as they themselves lived in a country where caste defined their identities. Even on this issue of caste they were silent. Here it seems that Indian Baptists focused on survival, and therefore never raised this issue in any of its brochures or newsletters.

It is difficult to understand why John Rangiah did not protest in any of his writings or sermons against racism. After all he was theologically trained by American Baptist missionaries in India who were socially conscious. In 1845 the American Baptist Missionary Society, the society that sent missionaries to India and was responsible for the theological training of Rangiah, differed with conservative Baptists on the issue of missionaries as slaveholders.[97]

One might speculate that he respected his white landlord, whom he described as "a benevolent liberal-minded person." At Rangiah's base in Kearsney, the indentured laborers on Sir James Hulett's estate were treated with more respect than their fellow Indians *in other parts of Natal*. Was this a case of his employer treating Rangiah well with the expectation that Rangiah would be loyal and subordinate? Taylor[98] states that subordination can provide control over the silenced subjects. Given the fact that Sir James Hulett was Rangiah's landlord who gave him a house to live in, as well as providing employment to the indentured Baptists on his tea estate, Sir Hulett did have power and control over Rangiah, which may have played a role in silencing Rangiah on the race issue.

As mentioned earlier, Rangiah was a conservative Baptist and thus reflected a conservative theology, which did not address the socio-political issues of his time. The leaders who followed were largely trained in institutions that did not take seriously those issues. However in the early 1990s, a few of the younger clergy in BASA began engaging in theological reflection focusing on socio-political issues. I myself attended a conference hosted by the BWA, called Baptists Against Racism, in Atlanta, Georgia January 8–11, 1999.[99] Baptist academics from around the world presented papers on the subject of race with strong criticism of race-orientated theologies.

Despite the progressive thinking of some of the younger clergy of BASA in recent years, BASA has not officially made statements condemning racism. I suspect this is due mainly to leaders' theological orientation.

---

97. Leonard, *Ways*, 200.
98. Taylor, *Altarity*, xxi.
99. Lotz, *Baptists*, 186.

During my leadership of BASA, my emphasis on the training of the leaders assisted them in acquiring knowledge and learning new skills, such as dealing with pastoral challenges regarding HIV/AIDS, preaching, women in ministry, and research. However, no significant progress was made in opening the organization to addressing the contextual realities, which would entail fostering race relations and intentionally seeking to bring other racial groups into its membership.

On the spiritual and cultural (and economic) fronts, the strategies employed by the leaders of BASA have contributed positively to the development of South Africa. However, the strategies employed by the leaders of the BASA have not significantly changed the organization's ethnic orientation. In 2006, BASA did not have a single Black church in its membership.

Thus, the response to the question, Did the strategy impact South Africa? is "Yes, it did, but mainly in the spiritual and cultural spheres."

The significant changes that have occurred in South Africa require the church to adapt to a new democratic South Africa. It will require the BASA to review its strategies in order to become a relevant faith organization in South Africa. What follows are suggestions to be considered so that BASA can move towards this ideal.

The BASA should move more aggressively toward the training of laity. John Rangiah's strategy of training laity was a significant hallmark of his ministry. Attempts were made later by the BASA Bible College to train its laity, and it did achieve a small measure of success during Anthony Poliah's term of office.[100]

I urge that BASA make a public statement on race. Since 1903 when the Indian Baptist Church was established and since 1914, when the BASA began its ministry, with the exception of the Baptist Mission of South Africa[101] Indian Baptists have not made a public statement on race. The late Martin Luther King Jr., a Baptist minister in the USA, took a public stand against racism in his country and today his legacy is an inspiration to many in the USA and around the world.

It should also make public statements on other issues. Generally, Baptists in South Africa have not made public statements on moral issues that affected the lives of millions of South Africans. The Baptist principle of the separation of church and state, it seems, may have prevented

---

100. Israel, letter.

101. Daniel, *Brochure*.

them from making statements. This principle does not, however, prevent Baptists from challenging policies that affect them. Currently, programs on television that have "adult content" are shown. Young children, if not monitored by adults, are exposed to such content. BASA can register its complaint by using the appropriate channels.

Ron Sider,[102] a leading evangelical in the USA, states that political decisions have a huge impact—for good or bad on the lives of literally billions of people. Bill Leonard[103] states that with regard to religious liberty and Christian citizenship, Baptists were among the first to call for radical religious liberty in the modern state. Baptists in the BASA should allow their faith to impact the public domain, as well as the state.

Generally, pastors consider themselves functioning only as pastors. They are also theologians as they should be thinking deeply and complexly about God. Nathaniel recognized this in his approach to ministry. He engaged the biblical text and presented complex issues to his audiences.[104] BASA pastors must embrace the legacy of Nathaniel, remembering that during his tenure, BASA grew significantly.

The function of the pastor as a theologian will help in the area of theological reflection. Pyle and Seals[105] explain this important issue: "Theological reflection occurs when the events of life are examined through the eyes of faith, in order to integrate experience and faith." The changing political and social landscape in South Africa requires that the pastor engage in theological reflection on issues of inter-race relationship, globalization, community development, and social ministries. Neil Sims quotes Geoff Thompson[106] on the importance of theological reflection by stating, "As such it is indispensable for the church's mission of worship, witness and service, not least in witnessing to the truth of faith before those who do not yet, or no longer believe."

The pastor must also be an administrator. Most of the churches in the BASA do not have the luxury of church offices and the services of office secretaries. Given this unfortunate situation, the pastor should be knowledgeable in office administration. This must go beyond just answering phone

---

102. Sider, *Scandal*, 21.
103. Leonard, *Ways*, 9.
104. Rangiah, *NIBA News*, 48–53.
105. Pyle and Seals, *Experiencing Ministry Supervision*, 110.
106. Sims, "Reflection," 15.

calls and sending e-mails, important though they are. The pastor must set ministry goals that are appropriate for his/her context and apply administrative skills to implement them. Theophilius Rangiah reflected this important element (i.e., the use of organization skills) in his pastorate.[107]

For many years the church has debated whether it should focus on physical needs or spiritual needs of the church. American Baptist missionaries such as Samuel Day, Lyman Jewett, and others engaged in a missionary enterprise in India that included the building of the Telugu community. They established schools and hospitals for the poor in India where they practiced social ministries.[108] Although in 1904 John Rangiah[109] established a school in Kearsney, in later years the BASA did not pursue the ministry of community development. One important ministry that calls for action is ministry to people living with HIV/AIDS. According to a 2007 report[110] 18.10 percent of people in South Africa between the ages fifteen and forty-nine are living with HIV/AIDS. BASA should develop a denominational ministry plan to minister to these people.

My goal has been to address the underrepresentation of the Baptist Association of South Africa in this history of Baptists in South Africa. This narrative was written from "the underside," i.e., from the point of view of the victim. This study has hopefully given new meaning and offered an understanding of events from a perspective different from the colonial perspective.[111]

---

107. Rangiah, *NIBA News*, 37.
108. Downie, *Lone Star*, 4–46.
109. Rangiah, *NIBA News*, 16.
110. Central Intelligence Agency, "Comparison."
111. Dharamraj, *Colonialism and Mission*, xi.

Bibliography

American Baptist Church. "Who we are." Office of Communication, 1988. No pages. Online: http://www.abc-usa.org/whoweare/vision/vision.aspx.

Baker, J. M. *Contending the Grade in India*. Asheville, USA: Biltmore, 1947.

Baptist World Alliance. Member Body Statistics. No pages. Online: http://www.bwanet.org/bwa.php?site=Resources&id=168.

Batts, H. J. *History of the Baptist Church in South Africa*. Cape Town: Maskew Miller, 1920.

Bhana, S. *Essays on Indentured Indians in Natal*. Leeds: Peepal Tree, 1991.

Birch, William. "The Sovereignty of God and Humanity's Free Will." Society of Evangelical Arminians. 18 August 2008. Online: http://www.evangelicalarminians.org/node/78.

Borthwick, P. *A Mind for Missions: 10 Ways to Build Your World Vision*. Colorado Springs: Navpress, 1987.

Bosch, D. Introduction to *Quest for Belonging*, by Inus Daneel. Gwero: Mambo, 1987.

Brauch, M. "The Theology of Marriage and Family." Professional paper 1, class lecture, Pennsylvania, 2–4 January 2007.

Carey, William. *Memoir*. Boston: Gould, Kendall & Lincoln, 1836.

Central Intelligence Agency. "Country Comparison: HIV/AIDS Prevalence Rate." In *The World Factbook 2009*. Washington, DC: Central Intelligence Agency, 2009. No pages. Online: https://www.cia.gov/library/publications/the-world-factbook/index.

The Coalition for Baptist Principles. "The Judson Declaration." New York: The Coalition for Baptist Principles, 2004. No pages. Online: http://www.baptistprinciples.org/declaration.htm.

Cornell, Stephen E., and Douglas Hartmann. *Ethnicity and Race: Making Identities in a Changing World*. Newbury Park, CA: Pine Forge, 1998.

Daniel, P. *Deep River Consultation Brochure*. Durban, 1993.

Davenport, T. R. H. *South Africa: A Modern History*. Johannesburg: MacMillan South Africa, 1977.

Dayadarum, C. "The Role of John and Theophilus M. Rangiah in the Baptist Missionary Enterprise among Asian Indians in South Africa." PhD diss., Ohio State University, 2001.

De Gruchy, J. W. *The Church Struggle in South Africa*. Grand Rapids: Eerdmans, 1979.

Dew, Diane. "Visions and Dreams." Milwaukee: Diane Dew, 1997. No pages. Online: http://www.dianedew.com/visions.htm.

Dharmaraj, J. *Colonialism and Christian Mission: Postcolonial Reflections*. Delhi: Indian Society for Promoting Christian Knowledge, 1993.

Dhupelia-Mesthrie, U. *From Cane Fields to Freedom: A Chronicle of Indian South African Life*. Cape Town: Kwela, 2000.

Dictionary.com. Dictionary.com, LLC, 2011. No pages. Online: http://dictionary.reference.com.

Downie, D. *From the Mill to the Mission Field*. Philadelphia: Judson, 1928.

———. *The Lone Star: The History of the Telugu Mission of the American Baptist Missionary Union*. Philadelphia: American Baptist Publication Society, 1893.

Dvorin, E. P. *Racial Separation in South Africa: An Analysis of Apartheid Theory*. Chicago: University of Chicago Press, 1952.

Dyrness, William A., and Veli-Matti Kärkkäinen. *Global Dictionary of Theology*. Nottingham: Inter-Varsity, 2008.

Elphick, R., and R. Davenport. *Christianity in South Africa: A Political, Social and Cultural History*. Oxford: James Currey, 1997.

Elwell, W. A. *Handbook of Evangelical Theologians*. Grand Rapids: Baker, 1984.

Elliot, R. H. "American Baptist: A Unifying Vision Study Document. The Ministers Council." 2005. No pages. Online: http://www.ministerscouncil.com/Clergy%20Congregation%20Resources/UnifyingVisionStudyDocument.aspx.

Escobar, Samuel. *The New Global Missions: The Gospel from Everywhere to Everyone*. Downer's Grove, IL: InterVarsity Press, 2003.

Ferguson-Davie, C. J. *The Early History of Indians in Natal*. Johannesburg: South African Institute of Race Relations, n.d.

Fitzgerald, J. *Cracks in an Earthen Vessel: An Examination of the Catalogues of Hardships in the Corinthian Correspondence*. SBLDS 99. Atlanta: Scholars Press, 1988.

Foucault, M. *Power/Knowledge*. Translated by Colin Gordon. Sussex: Harvester, 1980.

The Free Dictionary. Huntingdon Valley, PA: Farlex, 2011. No pages. Online: http://www.thefreedictionary.com/.

Goss, Greg. "Principles of Missions." Online: http://www.npchurch.org/adulted/studies/missions/missionlesson6.pdf.

Heesen, David R. "Isms, Shisms & Altar Calls." *Kingdom Digest*. No pages. Online: http://beloit.edu/~heesendr/Moody.html.

Henning, C. G. *The Indentured Indian in Natal: (1860-1917)*. New Delhi: Promilla & Co., 1993.

Hexham, Irving. *The Irony of Apartheid: The Struggle for National Independence of Afrikaner Calvinism against British Imperialism*. New York: Edwin Mellen, 1981.

Hoffmeister, D., and B. Gurney. *National Awareness Workshop*. Johannesburg: Awareness Campaign of the BCSA, 1990.

"Homelands." *South African History Online*. No pages. Online: http://www.sahistory.org.za/pages/places/villages/homelands/homelands.htm.

Hudson-Reed, Sydney. *By Taking Heed*. Roodepoort: Baptist, 1983.

"Indigenous church mission theory." No pages. Online: http://en.wikipedia.org/wiki/Indigenous_church_mission_theory.

Isichei, Elizabeth. *A History of Christianity in Africa: From Antiquity to the Present*. London: SPCK, 1995.

Israel, N. M. *Indian Baptist History: BASA Annual Brochure*. Stanger, KwaZulu Natal: Baptist Association of South Africa, 1988.

———. "John Rangiah and a Century of Indian Baptist Work in Africa (1903–2003)." Speech delivered to Baptist World Alliance Heritage and Identity Commission, Washington, VA, 2004.

———. Letter to Author. 1 February 1992. Personal Archives, Tongaat

Jacob, V. C., and H. Cornelius. *The Indian Baptist Mission Golden Jubilee Brochure, 1903–1953.* Durban: CP Press, 1953.

Jewett, F. *Leaves from the Life of Lyman Jewett.* Philadelphia: American Baptist Publication Society, 1898.

Jewett, L. *John Rangiah, The First Telugu Foreign Missionary.* Boston: American Baptist Foreign Mission Society, 1913.

Joshi, Barbara R. *Untouchables: Voices of the Dalit Liberation Movement.* London: Zed, 1986.

Kalu, Ogbu, ed. "Changing Tides: Some Currents in World Christianity at the Opening of the Twenty-First Century." In *Interpreting Contemporary Christianity: Global Processes and Local Identities.* Grand Rapids / Cambridge: Eerdmans, 2008.

Kinghorn, Johann. *Christianity Amidst Apartheid: Selected Perspectives on the Church in South Africa.* Compiled by Martin Prozesky. New York: St. Martin, 1990.

Kretzchmar, L. *Privatization of the Christian Faith: Mission, Social Ethics and the South African Baptists.* Ghana: Legon Theological Studies Series, 1998.

Lauren, Paul Gordon. *Power and Prejudice: The Politics and Diplomacy of Racial Discrimination.* Boulder: Westview, 1988.

Leonard, B. J. *Baptist Ways: A History.* Valley Forge: Judson, 2003.

Lerrigo, P. H. J., and Doris M. Amidon. *All Kindred and Tongues.* New York: American Baptist Foreign Mission Society and Woman's American Baptist Mission Society, 1940.

Lipphard, William B., et al. *Overseas: An Illustrated Survey of the Foreign Mission Enterprise of Northern Baptists.* New York: American Baptist Foreign Mission Society and Woman's American Baptist Foreign Mission Society, 1930.

Lotz, D. *Baptists Against Racism and Ethnic Conflict.* Mclean, VA: Baptist World Alliance, 1999.

Loubser, J. A. *The Apartheid Bible: A Critical Review of Racial Theology in South Africa.* Cape Town: Maskew Miller Longman, 1987.

Lloyd-Jones, D. Martyn. *God's Way of Reconciliation: Exposition of Ephesians 2.* Grand Rapids: Baker, 1972.

MacMillan, Margaret. *Dangerous Games: The Uses and Abuses of History.* New York: Modern Library, 2009.

"Mangosuthu Buthelezi." No pages. Online: http://en.wikipedia.org/wiki/Mangosuthu_Buthelezi.

Marger, M. N. *Race and Ethnic Relations: American and Global Perspectives.* Belmont, CA: Wadsworth, 2003.

Marsh, C. R., ed. *American Baptist Review.* Bezwada: American Baptist Telugu Mission, 1915.

McGavran, Donald A. *Understanding Church Growth.* Grand Rapids: Eerdmans, 1980.

McGrath, A. *Christian Theology: An Introduction.* Oxford: Blackwell Publishing, 2001.

Milton, Gordon. *Assimilation in American Life: The Role of Race, Religion, and National Origins.* New York: Oxford University Press, 1964.

Moodley, E. J. *Shembe, Ancestors, and Christ: A Christological Inquiry with Missiological Implications.* Eugene, OR: Pickwick, 2008.

Mogashoa, M. H. *South African Baptists and Finance Matters (1820–1948)*. Vol. 1. Durban: University of Kwa Zulu Natal, 2004.

Moses, K. D. *Indian Baptist Mission Diamond Jubilee, 1903–1978*. Brochure. Durban: Colortel, 1978.

Muthaiah, P. "Dandora: The Madiga Movement for Equal Identity and Social Justice." *Social Action* 54:2 (2004) 184–209. Online: http://www.simoncharsley.co.uk/rival.html.

Naidoo, B. *Rekindling the Fire*. Durban: Kairos, 2003.

Nathaniel, D. N. *The Origin of the Indian Baptist Church in South Africa 1900–1978*. Durban: University of Durban Westville, 1979.

———. *For the Preacher in the Making*. Durban: Mercantile Printing Works, 1960.

Nathaniel, V. P. Letter to BUSA. 1 February 1992. Personal Archives, Tongaat.

Ngcokovane, C. M. *Apartheid in South Africa: Challenge to Christian Churches*. New York: Vantage, 1984.

Neil, S. C. *World Book Encyclopedia*. Vol. 3. Chicago: World Book Inc., 1953.

Nicholls, Bruce J. *Contextualization: A Theology of Gospel and Culture*. Vancouver: Regent College Publishing, 2003.

Nussbaum, Stan. *A Reader's Guide to Transforming Mission: A Concise Accessible Companion to David Bosch's Classic Book*. New York: Orbis, 2005.

Olson, R. "Does Evangelical Theology Have a Future?" *Christianity Today* 42:2 (1998).

Oosthuizen, G. C., and I. Hexman. *Afro-Christian Religion at the Grassroots in Southern Africa*. Vol. 19. New York: Edwin Mellen, 1991.

Oxford Dictionaries. New York: Oxford University Press, 2011. Online: http://www.oxforddictionaries.com/.

Palmer, M. *The History of Indians in Natal*. New York: Oxford University Press, 1957.

Park, A. S. *Racial Conflict and Healing: An Asian-American Theological Perspective*. Maryknoll, NY: Orbis, 1996.

Paul, H. T. "From Telugu Baptist Church to Open Church: A Study of the Indian Baptist Missionary Enterprise in South Africa (1903–1989)." PhD diss., University of Durban-Westville, 1990.

———. "The Pentecostal Churches in the Vicinity of Stanger with Special Emphasis on the Indian Community." Master's thesis, University of Durban-Westville, 1987.

Polak, H. S. L., et al. *Mahatma Gandhi*. London: Odhams, 1949.

Power, C. "Gospel for Asia." *About Dalits and the Caste System*. No pages. Online: http://www.gfa.org/dalit/the-caste-system/.

Pyle, William T., and Mary Alice Seals. *Experiencing Ministry Supervision: A Field-Based Approach*. Nashville: Broadman & Holman, 1995.

Ragwan, R. *In His Service: A Faith Journey of a South African Pastor*. Durban: Kairos, 2003.

Rangiah, J. *The First and Second Annual Reports of the Telugu Baptist Mission, Natal, South Africa*. Madras: M.E. Press, First Missionary to the Telugus in Natal, South Africa, 1905.

———. *Missions: Impressions of the World Conference*. Vol. 9. Boston: American Baptist Missionary Union, 1910.

———. *The Telugu Mission in South Africa*. Valley Forge: American Baptist Historical Society, Africa, 1905.

———. *The Third Annual Report of the Telugu Baptist Mission, Natal, South Africa*. Cuttack: Orissa, American Baptist Historical Society, Africa, 1907.

Rangiah, M. *Natal Indian Baptist Association Golden Jubilee Souvenir Brochure 1914–1964.* Clairewood: Mercantile, 1964.

———. *NIBA News.* Clarewood: Mercantile, 1953.

Regehr, E. *Perceptions of Apartheid: The Churches and Political Change in South Africa.* Scotsdale, PA: Herald, 1979.

Ross, Kelley L. "The Caste System and the Stages of Life in Hinduism." *The Proceedings of the Friesian School, Fourth Series.* No pages. Online: http://www.friesian.com/caste.htm.

Shenston, T. S. *Teloogoo Mission Scrap Book.* Brantford: Expositor, 1888.

Sherring, M. A. *The History of Protestant Missions in India.* London: Religious Tract Society, 1884.

Sider, R. *The Scandal of Evangelical Politics: Why are Christians Missing the Chance to Really Change the World?* Grand Rapids: Baker, 2008.

Simmons, James Samuel, Jr. "An Inquiry into the Correlation between Theology and Mission as Illustrated in the History of the American Baptist Churches in the USA." PhD diss., Mid-America Baptist Theological Seminary, Alabama, 1989.

Sims, Neil. "Theological Reflection: A Purposeful Conversation." *Arché: The Annual eReview of the Brisbane College of Theology* (2005). No pages. Online: http://www.bct.edu.au/Arche/Sims.pdf.

Southern Baptist Convention. "About Us." Online: http://www.sbc.net/aboutus/default.asp.

Stack, Louise, and Don Morton. *Torment to Triumph in South Africa.* New York: Friendship, 1976.

Stanley, B. *The World Missionary Conference, Edinburgh 1910.* Grand Rapids / Cambridge: Eerdmans, 2009.

Srinivas, M. N. *Caste in Modern India.* New York: Asia Publishing House, 1962.

Subbamma, B. V. *New Patterns for Discipling Hindus.* South Pasedena: William Carey Library, 1970.

Sugirtharajah, R. S. *Asian Biblical Hermeneutics and Post-colonialism: Contesting the Interpretations.* New York: Orbis, 1998.

Swamy, R. *The Baptist Association of South Africa Annual Brochure.* Stanger, KwaZulu Natal: Victory Printers, 1999.

Taylor, J. D. "The African Church." In *Christianity and the Natives of South Africa.* Lovedale: Mission Conference of South Africa, 1928.

Taylor, M. *Altarity.* Chicago: University of Chicago Press, 1987.

Timothy, N. *Risecliff Baptist Church, Silver Jubilee of Rev. D. N. Nathaniel's Witness in South Africa, 1951–1976.* Souvenir Brochure. 1976.

———. *The Diamond Jubilee of the Indian Baptist Work in South Africa 1903–1978.* 1978.

"Tricameral Parliament." *South African History Online.* No pages. Online: http://www.sahistory.org.za/pages/library-resources/official%20docs/tricameral-parliament.htm.

Villa-Vicencio, C. *Trapped in Apartheid.* New York: Orbis, 1988.

Wang, J., ed. *Mission from the Third World: A World Survey of Non-Western Missions in Asia, Africa and Latin America.* Singapore: Church Growth Center, 1973.

Wilson, M. H. "Co-operation and Conflict: The Eastern Cape Frontier." In *Oxford History of South Africa,* Oxford: Clarendon, 1969.

Yohannan, K. P. "About Dalits and the Caste System." *Gospel for Asia.* No pages. Online: http://www.gfa.org/dalit/the-caste-system/.

"Zulu." Madison: National African Language Resource Center, n.d. No pages. Online: http://lang.nalrc.wisc.edu/nalrc/resources/press/brochures/zulu.pdf.

MINUTES

BRBM Minutes, 9 April 1999.
Bulwer Road Consultation Minutes, 19 February 1999.
Colesberg Minutes, 14–15 May 1998.
Rosebank Minutes, 18 November 1995.
SABA Minutes, 2 July 1999; 31 March 2000; 20 April 2001; 15 June 2001; 25 January 2002; 27 July 2002; 23 May 2003; 31 October 2003.

www.ingramcontent.com/pod-product-compliance
Lightning Source LLC
Chambersburg PA
CBHW071435160426
43195CB00013B/1915